"Saravá! Afro-Brazilian Magick *prov[...]* *important aspect of Brazil that is oft[...]* *the descriptions of Brazilian culture.*"

— Dr. Ralph Kite, former Chairman,
Department of Spanish and Portuguese
University of Colorado–Boulder

AN INSIDER'S LOOK AT A RELIGION ...
A CULTURAL FORCE ...
AND A POWERFUL MAGICKAL SYSTEM

Born in turn-of-the-century Brazil, the vibrant magickal religion of Umbanda combined ecstatic African traditions with European Spiritualism. Now you will discover, for the first time in the English language ...

- The powers of the Orixás, the gods of the Afro-Brazilian pantheon, and some of their fascinating legends
- What happens in the place of worship, the organization of the temples, and the identity of the devotees
- The spellwork and rituals, trance and mediumship, healing, and the secrets of the rites
- A quick reference guide to the Orixás showing the African meanings of their names, their Roman Catholic names, their dominions, dress, dance steps, and colors
- The tropical botanicals used in Brazilian magick and medicine
- Afro-Brazilian cuisine: the foods of the gods
- How to get personally involved in one of the sects
- Plus: a guide to Portuguese pronunciation and a glossary of Brazilian magickal terms

ABOUT THE AUTHOR

Carol L. Dow holds a Ph.D. in Portuguese and Brazilian Studies, and was the recipient of a Fulbright Dissertation Research Grant to Brazil. While living in Brazil, she researched Brazilian mystery religions, attended ceremonies, interviewed heads of sects, recorded music, and collected artifacts. *Saravá! Afro-Brazilian Magick* is the fruit of her work. She has a long, abiding interest in Brazilian mystery religions, and has lectured on the topic around the United States. She is currently translating a series of books on Macumba; the first volume, *Pomba-Gira* is already in print.

A Wiccan High Priestess, she is also well versed in Western Magickal Mystery Tradition. She has taught classes in Wicca for many years and has written books on Witches and the Craft under the name Morwyn.

TO WRITE TO THE AUTHOR

If you wish to contact the author or would like more information about this book, please write to:

Carol L. Dow
C/o Llewellyn Worldwide
P.O. Box 64383, Dept. K235-6
St. Paul, MN 55164-0383, U.S.A.

Please enclose a self-addressed, stamped envelope for reply,
or $1.00 to cover costs.
If outside the U.S.A., enclose international postal reply coupon.

Llewellyn Worldwide will forward your request. We cannot guarantee that every letter written to the author can be answered, but all will be forwarded.

SARAVÁ!

AFRO-BRAZILIAN
MAGICK

Carol L. Dow

1997
Llewellyn Publications
St. Paul, Minnesota 55164-0383
U.S.A.

Cover design: Lynne Menturweck
Cover photo: Leo Tushaus
Interior photos: Eric Witherow, Showcase Photographics
Interior illustrations: Tom Grewe
Editing and book design: Amy Rost

FIRST EDITION
First Printing, 1997

Library of Congress Cataloging-in Publication Data
Dow, Carol L.
    Saravá! : Afro-Brazilian magick / Carol L. Dow. — 1st ed.
        p. cm. — (Llewellyn's world religion and magick series)
    Includes bibliographical references and index.
    ISBN 1–56718–235–6 (pbk.)
    1. Afro-Brazilian cults—Brazil. 2. Brazil—Religion. 3. Magic—
Brazil.   I. Title. II. Series: Llewellyn's world religion & magic
series.
BL2590.B7D68   1997
299' .6' 0981—dc21   96-52081
                                              CIP

Llewellyn Publications
A Division of Llewellyn Worldwide, Ltd.
P.O. Box 64383
St. Paul, Minnesota 55164-0383
U.S.A.

This book is dedicated to Courtney Willis
in appreciation for his encouragement and support
in my studies of Afro-Brazilian sects over the years.

OTHER BOOKS BY THE AUTHOR

As Morwyn

Secrets of a Witch's Coven (Whitford Press/Schiffer Publishing, 1988)

Web of Light: Rites for Witches in the New Age
(Schiffer Publishing, 1993)

Green Magic (Schiffer Publishing, 1994)

Witch's Brew: The Secrets of Scents (Schiffer Publishing, 1995)

As Carol L. Dow

*Pomba-Gira: Rituals to Invoke the Formidable
Powers of the Female Messenger of the Gods*
(Technicians of the Sacred, 1990)

CONTENTS

	Photos	viii
	Illustrations	ix
Preface	Salve Todas as Nações!	xi
	Author's Note	xiv
Chapter 1	Brazilian Mystery Religions: An Overview	1
Chapter 2	Axé: The Powers of the Orixás	21
Chapter 3	Formidable Entities	49
Chapter 4	Believers and Their Sacred Ground	77
Chapter 5	Unique Practices	99
Chapter 6	Healing	139
Afterword	Saravá, Brazilian Magick!	167
Appendix A	A User-Friendly Guide to Portuguese Pronunciation	171
Appendix B	Personas of the Orixás	177
Appendix C	Some Tropical Botanicals Used in Brazilian Magick	186
Appendix D	Foods of the Gods	214
Appendix E	Music of the Spheres	222
	Glossary of Terms	225
	Bibliography	236
	Index	242

Photos

Typical ritual items sold in a casa de santo.   3

Spiritism founder Allan Kardec.   6

A berimbau.   17

Iemanjá.   27

Nanã.   29

Ogum.   31

Oxóssi.   37

Ossãe.   39

Xangô.   45

Two representations of Exu.   54

Exu das Sete Encruzilhadas.   55

Examples of Pombas-Giras.   57

Pretos Velhos.   61

The Caboclos.   63

Cabocla Jurema.   66

The adjá.   81

An example of a street ritual.   111

An altar cloth of Oxalá.   121

ILLUSTRATIONS

Figure 1   Layout of a typical terreiro.   93

Figure 2   Arrangement of objects on the altar
for an offering to Oxalá (for those born
under the zodiac sign of Leo).   118

Figure 3   Examples of personal sigils used for
invoking the Orixás.   122

Figure 4   More personal sigils for invoking
the Orixás.   123

Figure 5   How to cense a room to drive away
negative spirits.   153

Figure 6   The figa.   162

PREFACE

Salve Todas as Nações!

Salve Todas as Nações! Hail to all the nations![1]

White-clad figures sensually sway to an insistent drumbeat. Suddenly a dancer falls writhing to the ground and is carried away to another room—her eyes staring blankly, her body hanging limp and lifeless. Soon she returns to the dance floor, costumed like a gypsy in a flowing red-and-black skirt, a low-cut blouse, and heavy jewelry. She squats solidly on the floor; in one gulp, she quaffs a shot of strong sugarcane liquor, and lights a cigar. While she begins to blow smoke rings that rise leisurely into the air, she stares with unabashed curiosity at the audience.

A few members of the public tentatively and respectfully approach her to unburden themselves of their troubles and request advice in matters of love, money, health, protection, and even vengeance.

This vignette embodies the sexuality and exoticism that permeate the Brazilian magickal religions. These elements, along with other characteristics such as using folk healing and homespun therapy to overcome personal problems, form an integral part of the practices, because these sects are rooted in human experience.

Although this book addresses some seemingly exotic aspects of folk religion in Brazil, it primarily probes the spiritual roots of these sects and shows how deeply felt magickal beliefs affect all aspects of people's lives. Little is known abroad about the Brazilian mystery religions. The rites may seem eccentric to those accustomed to calmer religious fare. Nevertheless, *Saravá! Afro-Brazilian Magick* traces the common threads that tie these popular sects to Santería, Voodoo, Amerindian traditions, and even to European Positivism, Spiritualism, Roman Catholicism, and Western Mystery Traditions such as Wicca and Ceremonial Magick. Although Candomblé and Umbanda receive the lion's share of the attention here, other traditions—Amerindian, Macumba, Quimbanda, and Spiritist sects—are also discussed.

The book differs from those currently in print that either concentrate on personal experiences or present an academic viewpoint. *Saravá! Afro-Brazilian Magick* combines both approaches. Primary source material has been used whenever possible, and rituals and spells never before rendered in English have been translated. Also included is a large dose of personal anecdotes collected during my living and traveling experiences in Brazil, first as a Fulbright researcher, and later as a professor of Brazilian Studies.

The first chapter presents an overview of the tenets posed by several of these sects and shows the impact of these religions on the daily life of Brazilians. Chapter 2 describes the powers of the Orixás—the gods of the

Afro-Brazilian pantheon—and some of the fascinating legends surrounding them. Other uniquely Brazilian entities are examined in Chapter 3. What happens in the place of worship, the organization of the temples, and the identity of the devotees are the topics of Chapter 4. Spellwork and rituals, trance and mediumship, healing, and the secrets of the rites of these religions are revealed in the final two chapters.

A glossary of Portuguese/African terms explains unfamiliar vocabulary terms. A pronunciation guide is included in the appendices to help those unfamiliar with the Portuguese language. Other subjects covered in the appendices are a quick reference guide to the characteristics of the Orixás, tropical botanicals for magickal and medicinal uses, the food and drink offered to the gods, and the instruments that produce the incredible music with which the people honor their divinities.

Are you ready to launch yourself on an incredible journey? The Orixás are gathering to guide you. Just as the gods and goddesses are greeted, I say *saravá* to you. Welcome to the world of Brazilian magick!

NOTES

1. *Salve Todas as Nações!*—"Hail to all the nations!" *Salve* is a general expression of greeting to the gods when they descend to earth in the temple. *Nações* refers to all the groups of rituals brought by different African tribes to Brazil to form the various kinds of Candomblés. Instead of asking each other what sects they belong to, people refer to "nations."

Author's Note

Throughout this book, I refer to Brazilians of African decent as "Blacks" and Brazilians not of African decent as "Whites." In these days of political correctness in the United States of America, it should be remembered that this book is written about the United States of Brazil, where the current terms in use are Black (*preto*) and White (*branco*), and these terms are not considered derogatory.

Inter-marriage between races (miscegenation) has been practiced by the people of Brazil for centuries, including by the Portuguese who discovered and helped populate the country. Because of this, a wide range of mixed races has always existed in Brazil. To be technically correct, scholars in the fields such as sociology, politics, and economics use many terms to refer to the different racial combinations. Most Brazilians, however, call a rainbow of people either Black or White without any prejudicial undertones. Because I am writing in the Brazilian context, I choose to use the same terms Brazilians would select.

— Carol L. Dow

CHAPTER 1

BRAZILIAN MYSTERY RELIGIONS: AN OVERVIEW

It is a hot Friday night in Rio de Janeiro, and traffic swarms over the wide Avenida Atlântica that runs along Copacabana Beach. Oblivious to the frenetic movement around her, a well-dressed young woman on the median strip kneels in prayer over two candles, seven red roses, a cigarette, and an open bottle of liquor, all carefully arranged on a cloth. After meditating awhile, she rises and leaves the makeshift altar without looking back.

At a nearby cemetery, by the flickering light of a circle of candles, a silhouette with the face of a jackal crouches over a man bound tightly to a grave and blows smoke into the man's face.

In another part of the city in a run-down shack, ornately costumed dancers sway over a chalk-marked floor to a steady drumbeat.

In the capacious living room of a luxury apartment in the fashionable Barra da Tijuca district, a group of people gathers in a circle. Holding hands, they chant syllables of an unknown tongue as one of their number kneels in concentration over a single glass of water and carefully places rose petals around it.

Such scenes occur nightly throughout Brazil, and are manifestations of a belief in folk religion. While the state religion is Roman Catholicism, a general attitude of religious tolerance prevails; many Brazilians—far more than can be found in Hispanic countries—are tolerant of Judaism and Protestantism. Also, many Brazilians are either disciples of, or at least believers in, a related group of religions that go by the names of Spiritism, Umbanda, Quimbanda, Macumba, Catimbó, and Candomblé, just to name a few.

These unique faiths touch all aspects of Brazilian society and culture. Government and ecclesiastical sources estimate that there are around 300,000 centers where rites are performed. Even this is a conservative estimate, for it is often difficult to locate these temples. Those who actively participate in ritual magick are thought to compose approximately one-third of Brazil's 160 million inhabitants.[1]

One famous leader of the movement, Chico Xavier, a medium who used automatic writing to transmit messages from the world beyond, wrote more than 169 volumes of which more than five million copies have sold nationally—an astounding figure in a country with a fairly low literacy rate.

All over the country, shops called *casas de santo* (houses of the daint) sell articles for Umbanda/Quimbanda/Candomblé spells, including candles, baths, perfumes, colored ribbons, statues, glassware, clay pots, cigars, incense, jewelry, and literature about magickal religions. As recently as the 1940s, the government prohibited the sale of merchandise for rituals, and these establishments remained open under the guise of dealing in folk arts and crafts. Now that these sects have been legalized, shop owners do brisk business, though many stores are still tucked away from mainstream commercial life.

Small, often family-operated factories furnish the metaphysical supply houses with statues and other objects. One company in Rio, for example, employs fifty-five workers who produce 200 statues a day. The most popular images are Exus and Pombas-Giras (entities that look like male and female devils), Caboclos (Indian spirits), and Pretos Velhos (spirits of old Black slaves). (For a more complete discussion of Exus, Pombas-Giras, Caboclos, and Pretos Velhos, see Chapter 3.)

Folk beliefs are so influential that in the 1970s the Brazilian Roman Catholic Church was persuaded to change some of its policies[2] and now permits congregations to indulge in "pagan" practices such as

TYPICAL RITUAL ITEMS SOLD IN A CASA DE SANTO. *Top row: left to right:* sachet powder for spellwork, a talisman to bind a marriage. *Middle row:* loose incense in a bag, protection bath oil (large bottle), materials for a spell to bring good luck in gambling, discharge soap. *Bottom row:* pembas—colored chalk to draw invocational sigils.

kissing images; using drums, bells, and other musical instruments; energetically dancing in religious processions; and creating special ornamentation for altars.

Umbanda, the most widespread of these religions, has been active in local and state politics since 1960, when Átila Nunes was elected deputy to Congress and managed to have the religion legalized. In addition, many government and military leaders are rumored to embrace either the Umbandist or Spiritist faiths.

On any Friday night in Rio de Janeiro, numerous lighted candles can be observed on street corners, usually accompanied by food, cigarettes, matches, jewelry, and other offertory objects. To the uninformed visitor it appears as if mini-banquets have been carefully laid for unseen guests who never show up for the feast. Actually, these items have been left by believers, who, like the woman described at the beginning of this chapter, have consulted mediums at their *terreiros* (temples) about certain spells to be performed on street corners, crossroads, beaches, in forests, or by waterfalls, in order to persuade the gods to help them procure love, money, health, or perhaps satisfaction from an injustice.

These sects have produced some negative effects. For instance, a man from a slum recently stabbed his wife, mother-in-law, and two of his children, then flung another child over a cliff because they were all Catholic and did not believe in the spirit that imbued him. In another story, an itinerant worker from Bahia state in the northeast region became infamous when, in the name of his newly established Church of the Universal Assembly of Saints, he coerced several farm workers to relinquish their worldly goods and follow him aimlessly around the northeast. They eventually murdered eight of their own children by repeatedly driving them into the ocean until they drowned. One disciple explained, "God asked it to be so because the children were bad and would otherwise grow up to be delinquents."[3]

In one way or another, these beliefs suffuse Brazilian society and are reflected in music, art, cinema, and literature. For example, folk religion plays a predominant role in the later novels of Jorge Amado, an acclaimed writer from the northeast state of Bahia, whose works has been translated into English. In fact, Amado's novel, *Dona Flor and Her Two Husbands*, transformed into an enchanting movie, uses a scene from a Candomblé ceremony as a pivotal point of the action. The entire film is permeated with the flavor of magick as it is practiced in Bahia.

Contemporary Brazilian music also benefits substantially from interpretation of Umbanda/Candomblé themes and chants. Popular artists such as Gilberto Gil, Caetano Velloso, Jorge Bem, and Milton Nascimento incorporate traditional musical instruments into their music.

Brazilian magickal beliefs are organized into five basic religions, each with definable tenets:

1. Spiritism.
2. Umbanda.
3. Candomblé.
4. Macumba/Quimbanda.
5. Amerindian (east coast South American) traditions.

SPIRITISM

Spiritism is founded on the doctrines of the nineteenth-century French doctor and philosopher, Denizard, Hippolite-León Rivail (1804–1869), or Allan Kardec, as he dubbed himself. Kardec was convinced that spirits from the world beyond exist—some souls of the dead, others masters on the inner planes. They constantly endeavor to contact terrestrial beings in order to bring them messages of solace and lead us to the path of spiritual enlightenment. He believed that

Spiritism founder Allan Kardec. A bust of the leader surrounded by three of his works: *The Book of Mediums* **(left), two editions of** *The Gospel According to Spiritism* **(center), and** *Spiritism for Beginners* **(right).**

contact could be made with these entities through mediums. It was the mediums' solemn responsibility to prepare mind and body to receive these messages, and heal others with the power invested in them by the spirits.

Kardec outlined his theories in three fundamental works, *The Book of Spirits, The Gospel According to Spiritism,* and *The Book of Mediums.* To this day, Spiritists study the life and works of Kardec and accept no one else as a definitive authority.

Spiritism arrived in Brazil with Spiritualists[4] and homeopathic doctors of the latter half of the nineteenth century, and was patronized by Emperor Dom Pedro II and his chief minister José Bonifácio. Official sanctioning (more or less) of this religion by the modern powers that be have done much to spread its influence.

Spiritist worship services are elegant in their simplicity. Usually they are held in a plain room or chapel before an altar draped with a snowy white cloth, the only ornamentation consisting of two lighted white candles. Mediums wear simple white clothing, and unlike in the exotic rituals to be described later in this book, no drumming or dancing is condoned. There is always a sermon; sometimes chanting takes place in order to balance positive and negative energies. Mediums receive spirits and perform psychic healing. In a branch aptly called Table Spiritism, the mediums gather around a table to receive spirits in the manner of a Spiritualist seance. In Umbanda (described in the next section), the Spiritist tradition, or line, as it is called, has been deeply affected by Spiritist doctrine, although its practitioners, like other Umbandists, use drums, ornate clothing, and African rituals in their services.

One of the most attractive aspects of this religion is that for the Spiritist death does not exist. The individual merely passes on to a higher, more spiritual form of existence. Thus, Spiritism is a religion of hope.

Reading auras is an important part of Spiritist doctrine because an individual's physical, mental, and spiritual state, which is interpreted from the aura's color, reflects her/his progress on the path of enlightenment. While color is an important element of the other Brazilian traditions—as seen in the brilliant, beaded necklaces and costumes of the devotees—Spiritists limit themselves to using the power of colors only when reading auras. The colors are alleged to attract and transmit certain cosmic energies. The Spiritist explanation of aura colors and their meanings follows:

- Blue—spirit.
- Orange—ambition, pride.

- Red—passion, sensuality; dark red or pink—love, friendship.
- Green—treachery; dark green—jealousy, cupidity; light green—
  tranquility.
- Gray—depression, self-centeredness; dark gray—cheating,
  lying, hypocrisy; light gray—doubts, fears.
- Black—bitterness, revengefulness.

Although Spiritists do not not necessarily believe in the pantheon of gods and goddesses you will meet in the next chapter, and who form the backbone of the beliefs of the other Brazilian sects, the philosophical tenets of Spiritism have profoundly influenced the newer religions, such as Umbanda, Quimbanda, and Macumba, and have even made inroads into the more traditional faiths of Candomblé and the Amerindian religions.

UMBANDA

Probably the most familiar form of worship is Umbanda. One source[5] states that the name of this sect originated in Angola, where by the nineteenth century it had come to mean:

a. The art of consulting spirits of the dead.
b. The power of spirits to cure.
c. The art of coercing spirits to influence the living.
d. A type of fetish serving as a point of contact between
    the living and the dead.

Other Umbandists[6] insist that the term is borrowed from the Sanscrit word *aum-bandhu*, signifying "unity in trinity" and "the limit of the unlimited," or divine principle. Others point to a possible origin in the African word *kimbanda*, which means "priest," "doctor," "diviner," and "magician." What it has come to mean for Brazilians is the union of all the *bandas* (groups or rituals).

Other than these etymological definitions, it is difficult to characterize this sect. To attribute to it a potpourri of Spiritism, Roman Catholicism, European Witchcraft, Oriental, African, and Amerindian religions is somewhat facile, although it certainly does extract elements from all these faiths. The very complexity, individuality of interpretation, and elusiveness of Umbanda mark its distinctive character.

This uniquely Brazilian religion first appeared around the turn of the century. The Spiritist Tent of Our Lady of Piety was founded in Rio in 1908 by Zélio de Morais, a follower of Allan Kardec. During one session, the leader received the spirit of the Caboclo of the Seven Crossroads, who directed him to form seven more houses of worship with somewhat different philosophical tenets, which eventually became known as Umbanda. This marked the official beginning of the movement.

Theologian João de Freitas wrote the first book on the religion in 1939, and in the same year the Spiritist Federation of Umbanda was formed. (The federation changed its name to the Spiritist Union of Umbanda in Brazil eight years later.) The first Umbanda Congress met in Rio in 1941, where adherents sought to define its tenets and standardize the rituals of the sect. The leaders were not entirely successful in their attempts. Because such a wide variety of beliefs and practices exists today, Umbanda has divided into several traditions called lines.

As mentioned earlier, details of doctrine vary, but most Umbandists hold in common a belief in one creator god, whom they call Zambi. His lieutenants, who manipulate terrestrial life, are the *Orixás*, whom you will meet in the next chapter. Different lines cultivate some dissimilar Orixás, but generally Umbandists worship fewer divinities than do the other major sects, such as Candomblé.

Each Orixá commands a "line of vibration," or cosmic energy focus, which is subdivided into legions and phalanxes. These are governed for the most part by spirits of a lesser degree of evolution than the Orixás, but who are on a higher evolutionary scale than human beings. Offerings are made to these entities, and the entities take possession of the bodies of mediums through a process called incorporation. More about the lines of vibration is discussed in Chapter 5.

Umbandists also believe in spirit guides and protectors, elemental beings, the immortality of the spirit, reincarnation, the law of karma, and the act of ritual as a magickal expression and discipline.

Umbanda leaders have written guides for mediums that carefully outline a specific and restricted series of duties, responsibilities, and prohibitions. Practitioners agree that those who become mediums are bound to perform acts of charity both ceremonially and in their daily lives by mitigating suffering. Therefore, Umbanda signifies a way of life of love, dedication, benevolence, and renunciation of the material world.

Seven commandments of the Law of Umbanda must be memorized by all devotees. Translated, they are:

1. Do not do to your neighbor what you would not wish him to do to you.
2. Do not covet what is not yours.
3. Help the needy without asking questions.
4. Respect all religions because they come from God.
5. Do not criticize what you do not understand.
6. Fulfill your mission even if it means personal sacrifice.
7. Defend yourself from evil doers and resist evil.[7]

Besides the seven commandments for mediums, *filhos-de-santo* (cult followers) must attend all ceremonies; stretch out before their superiors with heads touching the floor in a gesture of obeisance meant to teach humility (known as *bater cabeça*, "beating the head"); help the leaders and their assistants; and wear clean, correct clothing.

Mediums must also behave in a dignified manner, not eat heavy meals, not consume meat from Thursday night through Friday, have faith in their spirit guides and terrestrial superiors, not share their knowledge or frequent other *centros*, and should never perform a service for anyone outside their own place of worship.

Punishments for breach of rules are meted out stringently by an administrative board. The punishments can include suspension for a number of days or weeks, expulsion, or the dreaded *tombo*—loss of official mediumship. In this case, the offender's laminated card with her/his picture and list of entities with whom the medium works is removed from its place on the wall of the center and destroyed.

Guilty parties often punish themselves, or, from their perspective, are mistreated by their spirit guides. After suspension from active practice, a former medium may attend a service and incorporate her/his entity. The entity then forces the person, who is in trance, to be thrown violently against walls, floor, and furniture. Spirit guides may even choose to *fechar a cabeça* ("close the head"), which is to prevent the transgressor from ever again incorporating an entity.

Umbanda is a generally middle-class religion, but people of all ages and from every sector of society and racial group participate. Since the 1920s and 1930s when Umbandists were persecuted and regularly incarcerated, Umbanda has become a legal religion, and as a result, an institutionalized religion. A Deliberative Council of Umbanda, a coordinating agency, and the Federation of Umbanda to which many of the centers are aligned, have been created to oversee the workings of the houses of worship.

The influence of institutionalization is also detected in the hierarchy of individual temples. The major figures, who are the spiritual and often also the administrative heads, are the male priest, the *Babalorixá*, and the female priestess, the *Ialorixá*. The spiritual and administrative hierarchies are discussed further in Chapter 4.

CANDOMBLÉ

The term *Candomblé* combines two words from the African Kikongo language, *ka* and *ndonbé*, which together mean "custom of the Black people." The Candomblé sects of Brazil, concentrated in, but not limited to the region of Bahia in the northeast, are credited with closely following the rituals of their African roots, or nations, as they are called. The religious traditions of the African Yoruba people (called the Nagôs in Brazil) are by far the most influential, affecting the Gegê, Keto, Oyó, and Indian Caboclo traditions. Even the African Bantu people, who gave rise to the Candomblés of Angola and the Congo, have felt the Yoruba influence both in their home country and in Brazil. The Yoruba came from what is today Nigeria. Their influence is said to predominate principally because of their numerical and cultural superiority and their highly developed language. Most of the African terms used throughout this book come from the Yoruba language.

According to oral tradition, three priestesses of the Orixá Xangô, Iyá Kalá, Iyá Detá, and Iyá Nassó, were transported by slave ships from Africa to Bahia in 1830 and founded the first real Candomblé terreiro, The White House of the Old Mill. From it were born all the great Candomblé houses of the city of Salvador, Bahia.

Candomblé has always been considered more "pure" in its practices because its followers attempt to closely mimic the African traditions. Sociologists and anthropologists[8] have been studying these sects since the turn of the century, and because scholars considered Candomblé a worthwhile subject, the people in general have validated this religion in their minds. Whether it is really any more or less genuine than any of the other, newer sects such as Umbanda, is a matter of opinion.

To the outsider, Candomblé rites may seem primitive and hampered by overly assiduous attention to detail. The more I learn about this religion, the more I appreciate the depth of philosophical knowledge it conveys through its subtleties of expression. In this opinion, I am not alone. According to Fernandes Portugal, a well-known writer of the Afro-Brazilian traditions, "The world of Candomblé is a very secret one into which a person only enters little by little...through a series of progressive initiations, specialized ceremonies open only to those called by the gods."[9] The myths of the Orixás, the music, songs, language, clothing, secret rites and public celebrations, even the cowrie shell divination (which relies on a philosophical system as complex as the Qabalistic Tree of Life) all combine to make Candomblé an exciting, deeply felt path of spiritual development. The true seeker on the path of Candomblé strives for "at-one-ment" with the godhead, as do those who follow the Western Magickal Mystery Tradition.

Differences between Candomblé and Umbanda, depending on the sect, can be vast or almost indistinguishable. In general, the followers of Candomblé adhere to the rituals of one particular nation rather than embrace an eclectic dogma as the Umbanda sects do. African languages are preferred over Portuguese in the ceremonies, and much of the doctrine remains secret. More Orixás are worshiped than in Umbanda, and some of the names for the deities are different. The spiritual leader may enjoy a certain amount of personal power when dealing with the Orixás rather than completely submitting to their will as is done in Umbanda. Less attention is paid to the Brazilian historical Pretos Velhos, Caboclos, and spirits of Oriental magi and children. Exu is simply a messenger of the gods, not an evildoer (see Chapter 3). Preparation for initiation can be a long and complicated process, and disciples may need to withstand severe deprivations, although this practice is changing due to influence from other sects and the necessities of modern life. There is always an altar reserved for the Orixás, hidden deeply within the recesses of the terreiro. Finally, blood sacrifices of four-footed animals and birds occur more often in Candomblé than in Umbanda.

MACUMBA/QUIMBANDA

Move the Candomblé cults to Rio de Janeiro and other southern cities, add a sprinkling of cultivation of one's ancestors, and dashes of Amerindian, Roman Catholic, European Occultist, and Spiritist influences, and out of the oven pops Macumba.[10] Some practitioners of the other religions denigrate Macumba because the *Macumbeiros* (devotees) tend to focus on the Exus and Pombas Giras, and perform spellwork for both good and evil ends. Fernandes Portugal claims that Macumba reflects the minimum amount of cultural unity necessary for people to show through their religion a sense of solidarity against a corrupt government and terrible social conditions. He says that "the Macumba of Rio has been perverted from its original intention. It has lost all its religious value and has ended up as a spectacle of Black Magick."[11]

Some Umbandists lump together the terms Macumba and Quimbanda (and claim that these should not even be considered religions). Author Vera Braga de Souza Gomes has said, "It does not possess a doctrinal basis—Christian or otherwise—its only purpose is to work magickal spells, it calls upon inferior spirits, and dedicates itself exclusively to doing and undoing evil."[12] (This, from an author, who four pages earlier in his book professes that Umbandists respect all other religions because they represent "paths of spiritual progress that lead to God.")[13]

On the other end of the spectrum, Macumba/Quimbanda proponents avow that these religions defy the White, capitalist cultural values of Umbanda by standing for the genuine liberation of the
downtrodden Afro-Americans.[14] According to these Quimbandists, the
priests and priestesses of Umbanda have become the indirect agents
of social and political integration, and were supported by the military
leaders during the times of the most recent dictatorship (1964–1985).
They argue that the Umbandistas are the ones who force the distinc-
tion between Quimbanda and Umbanda so that they can charge fan-
tastic sums to undo Quimbanda spells. Furthermore, they profess that
Quimbanda is both morally and politically more liberal than
Umbanda, and that "White" moral values are absent in Quimbanda.
They conclude that based on these assumptions, Quimbanda possesses superior magickal efficacy.

Perhaps an explanation of the contrasting beliefs of these sometimes warring sects may best be shown by using a parallel from the
tarot. In tarot divination, a card may be read right-side-up or upside
down, and some readers attach a specific significance to the card
according to its position. Other readers maintain that the meaning of
the card is essentially the same, and that a reversed card only means
that the reader should search for an interpretation from a less common point of view.

In the same way, Umbanda and Macumba/Quimbanda magick
may be seen as essentially the same phenomenon viewed in contrasting lights.

AMERINDIAN TRADITIONS

The indigenous tribes that the Portuguese found living on the land that was to become Brazil differed significantly from the highly developed civilizations of the Incas of Peru and the Aztecs of Mexico encountered by the Spaniards. The sparsely populated tropical forests of Brazil were inhabited by hunters and gatherers whose belief systems corresponded in many ways to those of the more highly developed African cultures whose people would later be imported as slaves to work on the plantations. For example, the Amerindians of Brazil worshiped one supreme creator/father/protector god, as did the Africans. They believed in evolved spirits, whose characteristics were roughly analogous to the Orixás, and who protected the forests and streams. They also admitted inferior entities who worked evil, like the Exus, Pombas-Giras, Eguns, and obsessed spirits. Like the Africans, they thought that some of their leaders could return to earth after death and render counsel to the living.

Unlike the Africans, they did not possess any visible manifestation of their worship such as altars, special clothing, or sacred images. They contacted their spirits through wild dancing and smoking tobacco and other substances during ceremonies led by the *pajé*, their spiritual leader who also cured with herbs like a *curandero* of the Hispanic traditions. During these rites, participants fell into trances and received the *encantados*, who are spirits, literally known as the "Enchanted Ones." The Indians developed their own collections of talismans, amulets, and fetishes, and performed *defumações*, "smokings" with tobacco and incense as a way to expel evil spirits from the body. They practiced natural magick with image dolls and divined the future by observing phenomena such as flora, fauna, and weather. Curiously, they also practiced a kind of cowrie shell divination, though not at nearly as sophisticated a level as the Africans.

Over the centuries, native beliefs have, to a greater or lesser degree, fused with those of the Afro-Brazilian system and have produced some definable traditions. The major sects are:

1. The Pajelanças[15] of the northern states of Pará, Amazônia, Maranhão, and Piauí—mostly a fusion of Amerindian and African beliefs with some weak Spiritist/Catholic influences.

2. The Xangôs[16] of Pernambuco, Alagoas, Paraíba, and Sergipe—mostly African with some Amerindian/Portuguese influence.

3. The Catimbós[17] of the entire northeast region—built on a blend of European Witchcraft and Portuguese folk traditions with some Amerindian elements mixed with Angolan-Congolese beliefs and shamanism from various sources.

Amerindian influences appear in Umbanda in some of the musical instruments and dances and the habit of purification with tobacco through smokings as well as in the cultivation of forest spirits, Caboclos, and other ancestors. Belief in the powers of spirits of animals such as snakes, alligators, and currasows (a kind of bird) has also had an impact on some Umbanda sects. I also think that the conception of Ossãe, the god of botanicals and curator of the forests, whom you will meet in Chapter 2, encompasses some native ideas that were different or absent in the African traditions.

A BERIMBAU. This Amerindian musical instrument is played during ritual dances. One way Amerindian traditions have influenced Umbanda is with musical instruments.

In all the sects described in this chapter, the music, dancing, and invocations produced during a ritual are designed to invoke spirit guides
and Orixás that descend into the bodies of the mediums. In the next
chapter you will meet the Orixás and learn of the awesome powers
they wield.

NOTES

1. According to Fausto Cupertino, a proponent of Roman Catholicism in *As Muitas
   Religiões do Brasileiro*, (Rio de Janeiro: Civilização Brasileira, 1976, 83), during a
   census poll taken in the mid-1970s more than two-thirds of the poor people living in city slums believed in the curative powers of the leaders of these sects, as
   well as in the efficacy of animal and plant sacrifices. More than 25 percent of
   those interviewed claimed to have experienced spiritual healing firsthand.
   Cupertino expresses a widespread Catholic opinion that laments the rampant
   spread of non-Catholic religions, like those discussed in this book, and Protestantism and Pentacostalism. He cites that about 100 years ago 99.7 percent of
   the population claimed to be Catholic in census documents. He says that the
   number of proclaimed Catholics fell to 75 percent by the mid-1970s, and that
   number has declined even further since that time, as can be seen by the decline
   in Catholic baptisms, confirmations, and marriages on the books. Although no
   current reliable statistics are available, given the recent growth of Protestantism
   and Pentacostalism and the strengthening of Umbanda, I would not be sur-
   prised if the real number of non-Catholics now approaches 50 percent.

2. The changes were made by the 1977 Itaicí General Assembly of Bishops of the
   Brazilian Roman Catholic Church, and appear in the liturgic *Directory for Mass
   with Popular Groups*.

3. The quotation is a translation of a statement made by Lourivalda Alves de
   Sousa, one of the fanatics, to the *Jornal do Brasil*, 1977.

4. Spiritualists are members of a religious group that came into prominence during the nineteenth century. They believe that the dead can communicate with
   the living through psychic mediums during seances. The medium either com-
   municates directly using the voice of the deceased, or relays information
   through automatic writing and drawing. The great Spiritualist hope has been
   to prove that life after death does indeed exist. The Spiritualist Association of

Great Britain still exists today at 33 Belgrave Square, Belgravia, London, SW1, England.

5. José Ribeiro, *Cerimônias da Umbanda e do Candomblé* (Rio de Janeiro: Editora Eco, 1974), 35.

6. Statement made by Lilián Ribeiro, Secretary of the National Deliberative Council of Umbanda to Atenéia Feijó, "Umbanda," *Gente*, May 1977, p. 102.

7. Many of these guides are published by Eco Press in Rio de Janeiro, e.g., Pompílio Possera de Eufrázio, *Catecismo do Umbandista* (Rio de Janeiro: Editora Eco, 1974).

8. Raimundo Nina Rodrígues, a physician by profession, was the first scholar to study Candomblé. Between 1896 and 1906, he wrote several articles on the subject, which appeared in magazines and journals. Even though he was of mixed race himself, Rodrígues believed that Afro-Americans were inferior to Caucasians, and that the people of African decent would never be able to integrate fully into Brazilian society. Artur Ramos, who came along in the 1930s, wrote a series of articles and books about Candomblé culture from a more balanced perspective, although he leaned toward psychoanalysis of the sects. In more modern times, the Frenchman Roger Bastide and Pierre Verger wrote several works that fully describe these sects.

9. Fernandes Portugal, *Axé: Poder dos Deuses Africanos* (Rio de Janeiro: Editora Eco, n.d.), 84–85.

10. The word *Macumba* comes from the Kikongo word *maku* and its past participle, *mba*, meaning "divination." In the interest of brevity, I have combined Macumba and Quimbanda in the text because the terms are often used interchangeably by laypeople to mean black magick. *The Dictionary of African Cults* defines Macumba as "a generic term for Afro-Brazilian cults modified by Angolan-Congolese, Amerindian, Catholic, Spiritist, and Occultist principles, practiced mainly in Rio and Minas Gerais State" (173–174). Quimbanda is rooted in a Kikongo term *kimbudu*, meaning "witch doctor." Quimbanda is an actual line of Umbanda that practices black magick, cultivates the Exus, Pombas Giras, and Omulu, and carries out rituals and initiations, in part, in cemeteries. Quimbandists work often with *pembas* (colored chalk), powders, animal parts, and herbs to create spells and offerings, which they "dispatch" at crossroads and other places. Quimbanda possesses seven lines, as does Umbanda.

11. Portugal, *Axé: Poder dos Deuses Africanos*, 101.

12. Vera Braga de Souza Gomes, *O Ritual da Umbanda: Fundamentos Esotéricos* (Rio de Janeiro: Editora Technoprint, 1989), 89.

13. Ibid., 85.

14. Marco Aurélio Luz and Georges Lapassade, one a sociologist, the other, a philosopher, put forth their theories in *O Segredo da Macumba*, (Rio de Janeiro: Editora Paz e Terra S.A., 1972). They represent a common viewpoint of many Candomblé followers.

15. The religion of Pajelança is named after the generic word for its priests who are called *Pajés*, or witch doctors. The followers of these cults worship the Enchanted Ones. Like members of the African cults, their mediums also fall into trances brought on, in part, by dancing, but also in part by using drugs. Some of the musical instruments like the maracas and rattles have influenced Macumba in Rio and the Caboclo Candomblés of Bahia.

16. The religion of the Xangôs is named for Xangô, the first African deity to set foot on Brazilian soil.

17. Possible origins of the word *catimbó* include the words of the Indian Tupi language, *caá*, meaning "forest, leaf," and *timbó*, meaning "poisonous plant." Also entering into the origin of the word is *cachimbo*, meaning "tobacco pipe." Those who practice Catimbó fall into trances by smoking marijuana, tobacco, and jurema tree leaves and bark.

CHAPTER 2

AXÉ: THE POWERS OF THE ORIXÁS

In African myth, when the great All Father, Olórun, finished creating the world and everything in it, He retired to His lofty realm for a well-deserved rest. In His place He left certain lieutenants who exercised His will on the material plane. These divine intermediaries between God and man are called the Orixás. This is why in the Yoruba language the name means "minor god," that is, a potency second only to the will of the All Father.

Actually, the Orixás represent the powerful vibratory forces of nature like wind, thunder, lightning, rain, and earthquakes. Their force is not crude, primitive, and aimless; they do not

21

expend their energies by performing mechanical actions like the elementals in Western Magick. The Orixás are spiritual entities of a superior evolutionary plane. Their powers can be cultivated, and, by virtue of their consciousness and intelligence, they can attend the calls of the faithful.

Their dynamic power, which is called *axé*,[1] can be concentrated into certain objects either by natural means, as in the case of plants, or by a concerted effort on the part of the faithful who, in special rituals that rely on sacrifice, invocation, and prayer, direct the vibratory energy into certain stones and metals. These charged objects, known as *assentamentos*, are buried under the center post that supports the terreiro so that the vital force of the Orixás will continue to protect and energize the temple.

Most followers believe that the Orixás evolved without needing to pass through incarnations in order to achieve perfection. Nonetheless, many of these deities have been syncretized with the Roman Catholic saints, who are believed to have led terrestrial lives. Syncretism occurs when two religions mutually influence each other to the extent that the characteristics of their gods intermingle and are confused, and eventually assimilate to form one entity. Before the Orixás were syncretized with Catholic saints, they suffered changes among themselves as the different African groups they represented found themselves thrown together as slaves in Brazil. Many Orixás from Yoruba and other Sudanese cultures, and the Bantu cultures, shared enough common attributes that the 400 to 600 original African Orixás were reduced to a couple of handfuls in Brazil. The assimilations are not always complete, which gives rise to the different, often contradictory myths surrounding the gods and shows why their characteristics vary from temple to temple.

The Orixás, as supreme lords of the elements of nature, exercise direct influence on humans, whom they are capable of protecting or punishing. Their powers can be manipulated through obedience, offerings, and incorporation (possession through the vehicle of a medium). Although the delegates' powers are limited to exercising the will of the Supreme Creator through His son Oxalá, the Orixás are extremely influential because they govern the course of human life at their discretion. Each possesses a positive and negative side, as do human beings, and like humans, they can behave well or badly. They kill and cure, protect and punish, love and hate. The Orixás are cultivated through their symbols, colors, modes of dress, representative beaded necklaces, dancing styles, drum rhythms, sacred songs, stones, and salutations. They are feared and respected, but also loved by their followers.

The explosive music and dancing that occur during a session help invoke both the Orixás and spirit guides to enter into the bodies of mediums for the transmission of healing and higher knowledge. Devotees do not believe that the Orixá itself incorporates into a medium, but that some part of the deity's powers is transmitted through a lesser evolved spirit that works for the Orixá. This is why a thousand Iansãs, for example, can descend into as many terreiros every night. (This concept is explained more thoroughly in Chapter 5.)

The first time an initiate is possessed he or she receives a spirit guide, and later, an entity of whom the medium becomes a *filho-de-santo*[2] (a devotee). Only temple chiefs can be possessed by all entities. Most mediums communicate with one to three entities in Macumba and Umbanda. In Candomblé they are allowed to work with only one. Although an entity's behavioral patterns vary according to the individual medium's personality, the changes are slight, and the same entity is easily recognizable regardless of the individual medium or tradition.

The purpose of this chapter is to introduce you to the Orixás. I begin with descriptions of each of the major Orixás who are cultivated in most terreiros, then follow with a legend that shows the deity's personality, origin, or philosophical significance.

In Appendix B, you will find a list of attributes that contribute to the building of each Orixá's persona, such as his or her characteristic dress, salutation for when he or she descends into the terreiro, and symbols. Elaborate rituals surround each deity, and the details of their expression must be followed to the letter. Nonetheless, inconsistencies plague these lists. For example, the colors, symbols, food, and modes of dress that are linked to each entity can vary slightly, depending on the sect or even the individual temple. This is because in the assimilation of the myriads of original Orixás, distinct traits have evolved for different oral traditions, and even within a sect, small variations can occur. Appendix B lists the attributes that surface most often.

IANSÃ

When the wind rustles through the temple, agitating the raffia that decorates the walls, the drums pause, and everyone looks around for Iansã to burst upon the scene. Renowned as the Goddess of the Fire Sword, Iansã ranks as the most temperamental, passionate, and vivacious of all the Orixás. Her pure energy dominates the winds and lightning, and she manipulates this power to provide cooling breezes, control electrical devices, and also to conjure up cyclones and tornados. Her scintillating sexual energy sparks unbridled passion, orgasm, jealousy, impetuosity, and free love. This haughty, demanding, irascible lady is the only Orixá formidable enough to handle the Eguns, the spirits of the dead, whom she cows with her flaming sword and *iruexim*, a whip fashioned from the hair of a horse's tail. In Africa, she is so ferocious that she wears a short beard, which she hides behind a small veil. This characteristic has not translated to her Brazilian persona.

Legend

The story goes that Iansã was a bright, intelligent, impetuous girl eager to know everything about the world. Because of her fervently sexual nature she chose to serve an apprenticeship (so to speak) by seducing all the male Orixás, and convincing them that in return for her favors, they should teach her their secrets. From Oxóssi she learned to hunt, and from his son, Logun-Odê, to fish. Ogum taught her to wield a sword, and Oxaguiã showed her how to use a shield for protection. Obaluaiê initiated her into the mysteries of the spirits of the dead. Even Exu let her in on the enigmas of fire and enchantment. However, when she set her cap for Xangô, she got more than she bargained for. Although he showed her the magick of thunder and lightning, she fell for him madly and irrevocably, and experienced the burning passion and heartache of love. From their union were born the Ibêji twins.

THE IBÊJI

I still remember my astonishment when I first saw a medium incorporate one of the Ibêji, the twins of the Afro-Brazilian pantheon. I could not fathom why this middle-aged woman was squatting on the floor like a little girl playing a game with a little ball, occasionally squealing in delight. She approached and raised her innocent eyes to me, calling me *tia* (aunt), and in baby talk begged me to bless her and give her a piece of candy, I was shocked. It took me a long time to understand that the true purpose of these cosmic mischief makers is to remind us of the power of laughter. With their jokes, infantile behavior, and giggling, they are able to undo the most powerful binding spells. Through the Ibêji, we remember to value the innocence and purity of our childhoods, thoughts of which can still bring us happiness and contentment.

The twins watch over children from the time they are babies and guide them until adolescence, regardless of the Orixá's authority with whom they are linked. Besides symbolizing happiness, childhood, and the lighter side of life, the Ibêji are associated with beauty, gracefulness, flowers, perfumes, and enchantments. Although they are syncretized with Saints Cosmus and Damian, the concepts they express really have no equivalent in the Roman Catholic belief system.

Legend

It is told that when the Ibêji were born, the last to leave the womb was actually the eldest; he was quick enough to back up and push his sibling out first so he could learn from watching the experience.

IEMANJÁ

Once a year on Iemanjá's feast day, the peace and serenity of this mermaid goddess enfolds the beaches of Brazil in her loving, protective mantle. On December 31 in Rio (February 2 in Salvador) the entire city migrates to the beach. Families and friends gather and carve holes in the sand, which they fill with lighted candles and flowers. They also construct miniature wooden boats and decorate them with flowers, combs, bars of soap, mirrors, and tiny perfume bottles. At midnight, as fireworks explode from atop the high-rise hotels to ring in the new year, the faithful holding vigil on the beach murmur prayers and launch the candlelit crafts into the sea. Then they immerse themselves in the foaming surf for a purification bath. In this way, people—whether they are initiates or not—commemorate the feast day of Iemanjá, the lithesome Lady of the Vibratory Force of the Sea.

Known as the Mother of Pearls Goddess, Iemanjá is perhaps the most beloved goddess throughout Brazil. Maybe this feeling stems from great affection for and loyalty to the family, a general value shared by most Brazilians. Iemanjá is the Orixá of pro-creation, gestation, and the family, and holds absolute reign over the hearth fire. When a baby is born, she makes sure it will live the normal life of a thinking, reasoning human being. She educates and raises children and instills in them respect for their parents and siblings.

IEMANJÁ. Goddess of the Sea and Mother of Pearls.

She teaches parents to love and care for their offspring as well. She presides over family reunions, weddings, birthdays, and anniversaries, and gives a person a sense of identity, a feeling of belonging. This value for kinship and group extends beyond family to friends, neighbors, and community. By analogy, many practitioners consider her to be the mother of all the Orixás.[3]

Legend

Iemanjá bore three sons: Ogum, Oxóssi, and Exu. All her children left home—Ogum to conquer the world, Oxóssi to pursue a meditative life in the forest, and Exu to see what the world had to offer. Only Exu returned. At first, his mother was delighted to see him. As they talked, he became agitated and finally blurted out that he had searched the planet in vain to find a woman to equal her perfection, and that because of his failure to discover one he knew he was destined to possess her and her alone. Then he grabbed his mother and tried to violate her. In the struggle, Exu ripped open her breasts. When he saw what he had done, he recoiled in horror and shame, and fled, banished from the kingdom of heaven, never to return. From the copious tears Iemanjá shed the oceans were formed, and from her torn breasts were born all the other gods.

NANÃ

If Iemanjá is the mother of the Orixás, then Nanã surely is the grandmother, because she embodies the First Great Force of the Supreme Law of Umbanda, which controls cosmic energy. Born of the tempest, she is considered the Mother of the Rain. Every time a devotee takes a bath, showers, swims, or in any way comes in contact with water, Nanã is remembered. When she incorporates, her mediums bend their bodies and walk slowly with frail steps supported on canes. This granny is a calm, ponderous, patient immortal whom it is difficult to annoy. However, be advised, anyone who really runs afoul of her temper had better watch out, as she goes blind with anger and strikes out at anyone in her path!

Nanã also merits the high rank of Guardian of the Portal of Death. In this exalted position, she reminds us that in order to experience life we must also understand death, for one cannot exist without the other. She is also the Goddess of Truth. Curiously, her cult was almost unknown in Brazil until this century, and she is gaining more and more followers every day.

Legend

Ogum was out roving the countryside when he happened upon Nanã's land. He knew he should have asked her permission to pass through her territory, but since she wasn't around and this warrior Orixá feared no one mortal or immortal, he proceeded on through. By-and-by, he came upon a marsh he had to traverse before he could leave her property. Suddenly, on the other side of the marsh, Nanã appeared—an ancient, white-haired grandmother bent over a cane.

Her voice quivered as she spoke. "Ogum, as you well know, you cannot pass through my land without asking my permission."

Ogum eyed the frail old lady and responded harshly, "As you, Nanã, well know, I ask permission of no one about anything. I go where I please."

Politely, she insisted, but he paid no heed. "Then," her voice took on a threatening tone, "I promise you will suffer the consequences, for I guarantee you will not pass through my land."

With a smile of derision, Ogum stepped defiantly into the marsh, but as he walked he sank deeply into the thick mud. Thrashing wildly with sword in hand, Ogum struggled with all his might, but still he sunk deeper and deeper into the morass.

NANÃ. Mother of the Rain and Guardian of the Portal of Death.

At last admitting defeat, he swallowed his pride and asked the granny's permission.

"Ogum, you are so fearless, young, and strong, but too impetuous," she said, as she shook her head and helped him extricate himself. "You need to learn to respect your elders."

Ogum, definitely a sore loser, hightailed it out of there, but not before he threatened that one day he would return and fill her marsh with pointed steel so it would cut her to ribbons if she set foot in it. To this day, Nanã's followers can wear no jewelry or anything else made from metal, for the goddess has banned that element from her kingdom.

OGUM

Ogum, renowned as the Orixá of war, is a kind of Mars/Aries figure. In the great battle of life, he is the field marshall.

The first time I saw a representation of this ferocious Orixá, I was changing money downtown at the Parallel Market (read "black market") in Rio. This unprepossessing little storefront on the Avenida Rio Branco looked just like all the other exchange houses in the vicinity, only here you got substantially more Brazilian money for your dollar. Of course it was illegal—well, semi-illegal—during the last dictatorship. From time to time, the military police (MP), when they didn't have anything better to do, "raided the joint" and closed it down just to keep the brokers "honest." Typically for Brazil, the exchange house would bounce back into business the next day, and also typically, the MP would turn a blind eye, at least for a while. Nervously waiting in line to exchange travelers' checks, wondering if "today would be the day," I glanced around at the spartan decor and spied a statue of an Orixá in a niche high on the wall. Ogum, shining in the light of a votive

OGUM. God of war, family, responsibility, and agriculture.

candle, surrounded by flowers and other offerings, astride his white horse and brandishing a sword at the door, defied the MP or anyone else with ill will to trespass the threshold.

Ogum represents the uncontrollably dominating force of movement. Although he is severe, war-like, rigid, and all-controlling (sometimes even to the point of cruelty), he is the most responsible of the Orixás. He strives to keep his family together safe and secure, and as such, proves a compassionate, understanding father figure, and a noble lord. In this capacity he commands respect as the guardian of agriculture and the black volcano, the forger of steel and iron.

Ogum's presence is felt at intense moments in life. He is the sharp cry of anger or pain, the clanging of the fire engine that shatters the stillness of the night, the sound of the jack hammer, the detonation of a bomb. His home is the automotive plant, barracks, arms factory, and workshop. He protects soldiers, construction workers, dentists, truck drivers, and anyone who must take a long journey.

Legend

One day after returning from a hunting expedition to feed his family, Ogum discovered his house in flames and his family threatened by warriors from distant lands. He flew into a rage, lunged at the attackers and destroyed them all.

Then he proceeded to teach his younger brother Oxóssi how to hunt in the forest. Ogum said to his brother, "The battle for the lives of my family has awakened my fighting instinct. I feel warrior blood coursing through my veins, and I know I must soon leave you to conquer other worlds. For this reason I have taught you the secrets of the hunt so you can provide food for our family in my stead."

As he turned to leave, he added, "Remember if you are ever in trouble, just call to me, and I will appear by your side in an instant to defend and protect you. No matter where you are I will fly to your defense." Thus, Ogum provides a paradigm for family responsibility and loyalty.

OMULU

An Orixá of many "faces," Omulu's physical visage is hidden by the straw mask that covers his face and entire body. His different names reveal his fearsome, multi-faceted nature. As the virile warrior, this Lord of the Earth is called Obaluaiê. As he personifies the heat of the sun and the energy of good health, he is called the Doctor of the Poor. On the other side of the coin, Omulu is an old man who covers his head with a straw hood called a *filá*. His face is covered to hide the smallpox scars that infected him as a child. It also shows that as the deity of death and contagious disease, he commands such respect that no one dares look upon his face. Those who seek Omulu's advice when he incorporates in his mediums tremble in his presence, for they know he presides over the mysteries of death and rebirth. His precinct is the cemetery, and he is Chief of the Wing of the Eguns. His ancient name, Xampanã, is so feared that it cannot be pronounced aloud.

Although Xangô is the volcano, the earth cannot erupt without Omulu's permission. His magick is so strong that only Nanã can contain him. Omulu visits illness, pestilence, and death on humanity, but he also works magick to help people stay healthy in their daily lives.

When a person takes a breath, speaks, or feels pain inside, especially in the bladder, the presence of Omulu is felt. Although he can cause skin diseases, evil humors, putrid smells, and insanity, he is also merciful. When a person dies, he guides the soul to the world beyond.

Legend

Omulu was abandoned by his mother Nanã in childhood because of the illness that scarred his face. Iemanjá took pity on him and raised him as her own child, teaching him how to cure infections.

One fine day while he was on a journey, he ran out of food and water. He decided to stop by a village and request sustenance. However, the residents, frightened by the specter swathed from head to foot in straw, ran him off. The Orixá then slowly retired to a nearby hill where he sat silently watching the rising sun.

As the solar disc climbed higher into the heavens the town's water supply dried up, crops shriveled, food spoiled, and the air hung heavy with putrid smells. Soon people began to feel nausea and were overcome by raging fevers. Some went insane; others died. After three days of searing sun and no night, the elders went to Omulu, who still sat in stony silence on the hill. Although they quaked in his stern presence, their need overcame their fear.

"Our crops have shriveled, our water's dried up, and we are dying of hunger, thirst, and disease," they lamented. "Oh, great Omulu, have pity on us!"

Suddenly Omulu stood up and without a word strode down the hill to the village. As he entered town, the water began to run pure again, the crops revived, and a cooling breeze lowered the temperature. The awesome deity moved through the lanes curing the sick, and even raised the dead from their shallow graves. The townspeople rejoiced. Then the Orixá again asked for food and water. This time the people feted him with the best they could provide. Because he had taken pity on them, they had learned to be merciful to others. Still, in some parts people are warned never to leave home in the heat of the day when the sun is high without covering their heads, so as not to incur the god's fatal wrath.

OLÓRUN

The Almighty God Olórun, known also as Zambi, created the earth, including man and woman, in four days. Then He made an alliance with humankind, which He expressed as Oxumarê, the rainbow that connects heaven and earth. After that, He retired to his celestial realm to rest from His labors. He delegated the authority for solving the mundane problems of earth to His lieutenants, the divine Orixás, chief of whom is His son, Oxalá.

In the Brazilian sects Olórun is only referred to in a general way during ritual prayers. He has no devotees, and is never incorporated.

OXALÁ

More than an Orixá, Oxalá is canonized as the father of the Orixás, and Chief of Planet Earth. Like Omulu and Oxumarê, he possesses two distinct forms, and also manifests a third, puzzling characteristic.

As the young god Oxaguiã, a noble warrior, he carries a *pilão* (pestle) wherever he goes. His second aspect reveals a bent old man Oxalufã, who supports himself on a cane that he thumps three times on the ground to determine the fates of humans' souls when they die.

Although syncretized with Jesus Christ, Oxalá typifies some ideas quite distinct from those symbolized by the Christian savior. He is the end of the road—the beginning of death. This is why he and his devotees always dress in white, the color of mourning. However, the end, as depicted by Oxalá in Afro-Brazilian doctrine, is not so terrible as some other religions would have us believe. Because death is inextricably bound up with life—life's ultimate consequence—one concept cannot exist without the other. So the death Oxalá offers is really the final rest, also known as peace. Peace, in turn, represents the positive equilibrium of the universe, the ultimate synthesis of humankind with the forces of nature.

As the embodiment of sanctity, Oxalá presides over purification ceremonies and inaugurates the season of public feasts. His followers change the water at his altar each day, replacing it with the purest, most undefiled liquid they can find.

Oxalá's puzzling characteristic is that although he is conceived of as the Father of the Gods and is married to Nanã or Iemanjá, he dresses as a woman. The following myth explains why.

Legend

As you know, Nanã is the guardian of the Portal of Death, and only she and her female followers are privileged to know what exists on the "Other Side." Oxalá was consumed with a burning desire to find out what lay beyond the portal, so he devised a plan. He dressed in a white skirt like a female acolyte and donned the *adê*, a traditional crown with beads that covered his face. Then he joined the procession of women wending their way to the portal. Just as he was about to glimpse beyond the threshold, Nanã discovered his identity.

"Aha!" she exclaimed. "Oxalá was so curious to learn my secrets he disguised himself as one of my followers! For your trouble, I declare that you indeed shall find out what exists in the realm of death, and with your cane you will decide the fates of all beings who pass this way. However, the price paid for gaining this knowledge and power will be always to dress as a woman and receive from your worshipers offerings of chicken and goat and other animals of the kind traditionally sacrificed to the female Orixás."

So it was that Oxalá came to be portrayed as a woman. His presence is felt at moments of great human anguish. As counselor and savior, he brings eternal, untroubled rest to humanity.

OXÓSSI

As you have learned, Iemanjá's contemplative son Oxóssi left home early to become Lord of the Forests and King of the Hunt. Now he perambulates the dense jungle, often in the company of Ossãe, Lord of the Plant Kingdom. He searches for items that possess good axé (spiritual force) and delivers them to the altars of the Orixás. By analogy, he represents positive energy, prosperity, and abundance. He is always present at meals and wherever any agricultural activity such as planting or harvesting takes place. His vital force permeates cleansing and purifying baths and incense smoke, for he diffuses and neutralizes negative energy. His energy can be so positive that he is often called the Lord of the Art of Living. He represents liberty of expression, optimism, and dynamism. As all the Orixás also express a negative side, Oxóssi's is that of the dreamer. His laziness can cause procrastination, shoddy work, inertia, and putrefaction. Although he bestows abundance, he can also incarnate paucity and famine.

Because he is a dreamer, idealist, and lover of all things beautiful, Oxóssi is considered the patron of the arts. He presides over all creativity, whether it be expressed in painting, sculpture, singing, planting, or procreation, and his genius is often called upon to inspire fecundity.

OxÓssi. Lord of the forest and the hunt.

Ogum taught Oxóssi to hunt, among other reasons, in order to shake him from his lethargic life. Then he learned about the forest and the secrets of botanicals from Ossãe.

Legend

Legend has it that Oxóssi originally was not a god, but a human being named Odé, who was married to Oxum. One day, he took it into his head to go hunting for the serpent, Ifá,[4] who actually was not a snake at all, but a divinity. Odé didn't believe that story.

When he found the snake in a tree, it sang out to him, "I'm not a creature that you can kill, Odé!" The hunter paid no heed, slew the viper, and stuffed it into his leather pouch. However, it kept singing even though it was dead. When Odé reached home with his catch, Oxum recoiled in horror and fled. Odé cooked up the snake anyway and ate it for dinner.

When Oxum returned the following day, she found her husband dead on the floor and the trail of a snake leading off into the woods. In tears, she ran to Ifá and pleaded for mercy. The God of the Ineffable considered the case, and decided to make Odé's body disappear. Seven years later the hunter reappeared as the Orixá Oxóssi. Sometimes confusion occurs between Oxóssi and his son Logun-Odê because of the similarity in the names given in the legend.

OSSÃE

Ossãe (also Ossaniyn or Ossaim), the son of Nanã and brother of Obaluaiê, Oxumarê, and Euá, was a pensive, introverted boy, who loved to study plants, take care of animals, and experiment with the curative powers of botanicals. Soon he left his home for life in the jungle, which he inhabited with Oxóssi. So thoroughly did he learn the mysteries of the axé of plants he soon became known as the Master of the Green and Father of Homeopathy. The axé offered by plants is indispensable to all rituals because it makes it possible for humans to call upon the Orixás and for them to descend to the terreiro. Without the benediction of Ossãe, no ceremony can take place.

The sacred verse that is chanted at many ceremonies in the Yoruba tongue sums up this great god's powers: *Kosi ewe, kosi orisà*, "Without leaves the Orixás cannot exist. Without leaves, there is no axé!"

As the Father of Homeopathy and the guardian of the axé of plants, Ossãe is a chemist and alchemist, the original witch doctor. His presence is felt wherever healing takes place—the temple, hospitals, doctors' and dentists' offices, pharmacies—and he protects all healers.

This omnipotent Orixá of the wild dresses in a green, white, pink, and brown calico skirt, and wears a red leather cap or plumed helmet. In one hand he carries a pestle with which he crushes herbs, and in the other hand he holds an iron or brass diadem with seven upward-pointing shafts and a bird at the center. His blue and white sash is belted in back, and his beads are milky white, red, blue, and green. He, of course, knows which herbs are best for humans to use in prestidigitation, but prefers to divine by ventriloquism. He is most often syncretized with Saint Benedict, and in his work he is sometimes helped by Dudu Calunga, a

OSSÃE. Lord of the Botanical World.

short, merry, one-legged Black man who plays a kind of harp called a *kora*. Anyone who hears the music falls under its spell and is transformed into a botanical, thereby enriching the fabulous world of the vegetable kingdom. Ossãe's salutation is *Ewê ô*, which means "leaf."

Legend

That Ossãe was privy to the secrets of botanicals irked Xangô, so he convinced Iansã to try to wrangle the secret out of the herbal divinity. The Goddess of the Winds went to Ossãe, and pleaded with him, but he remained impassive. In a fit of pique, she grabbed her skirt and shook it so hard that the leaves of the forest blew off the trees and scattered to the four kingdoms. Ossãe stood by watching her, still not uttering a word. In this way, vegetable life was spread to the four corners of the world.

Triumphant, Iansã returned to Xangô to brag about her success. Ossãe, however, was unimpressed, because he knew that though Iansã had physically disseminated the vegetation, he still was the only one who knew how to unlock the secrets of plant life.

Thus, Ossãe, whose name in Yoruba means "glorified morning light," confers healing, peace, tranquility, and harmony on the world. If his kingdom is devastated by those who would attempt to harness nature, he fights back by destroying the land.

OXUM

The youngest and most beloved wife of Xangô, Oxum is portrayed as the Orixá of sweet water, waterfalls, and brooks. Her energy is feminine and mild, sensitive and charming. When possessed, her mediums often behave like teenage girls, coquettish and sweet. They demand mirrors, little bells, combs, golden-colored objects, and conch shells—small vanities as rewards for their magick.

On her negative side, Oxum likes to provoke envy, gossip, intrigue, and deceit. She is so vindictive that in some myths she is accused of cutting off the ear of another of Xangô's wives, Obá, because she thought she was losing her husband to a new favorite. Not surprisingly, she is considered the most capricious and vain of the Orixás. This aspect of her energy sometimes approximates that of the Pombas-Giras (see Chapter 3).

As all the Orixás possess multifaceted natures, Oxum also stands for the true love of marriage. She is capable of calming the passions inflamed in men by Iansã, and makes them loyal, responsible husbands. She also oversees the development of the fetus in the womb and makes it strong and healthy.

In Bahia, she has become the goddess of petroleum, because the known bulk of the nation's oil supply lies offshore. Altars to her are erected there at the edge of the sea. In some contemporary, non-traditional cults, Oxum is confused with Oxumarê, the rainbow. It is said that originally Oxum was Oxóssi's wife, but he treated her so badly she went to live with Xangô. Her gratefulness to this stern god for becoming his favorite compensates for her jealous nature. Interestingly, of all the female Orixás, she alone is privy to the mysteries of the divinatory cowrie shells, as you will see below.

Legend

This daughter of Oxalá was a pampered young miss accustomed to getting her own way. She took it into her head that she wanted to learn to throw the cowries, a mystery jealously guarded by Exu, the only entity allowed to work with them. When she went to him and tendered her request, he laughed in her pretty face.

Determined to seek revenge, Oxum struck out into the deepest, wildest recesses of the forest where she found the witches who abide in the dense jungle. When she told them her story, they readily agreed to help her trick Exu. They gave her a magick potion, and she thanked them and left the forest, going directly to her nemesis.

"Oh dear Exu," she called, "would you like to see the treasure I found?"

Ever curious, Exu bent over her closed hand to see what she was carrying. Oxum threw the magickal powder into his eyes, blinding him. In his pain, he dropped the cherished cowrie shells he always held so close.

"Ay! Ay!" he screamed, "my dear little *búzios* shells are lost forever!"

"Not necessarily," the girl replied calmly. "Here, let me help you look for them. How many did you say there were?"

"Sixteen, sixteen," the entity quickly answered.

"How big is the biggest one, and what does the smallest one look like?"

In his desperation, Exu readily gave her the names, sizes, and shapes of the shells and their meanings in divination. At last, when Oxum had restored each cowrie to his palm and his vision had cleared, Oxum was long gone.

She hurried back to her father Oxalá, who was so impressed with the intelligence and artfulness with which she had wrested away Exu's secrets that he conferred on her the power and right to divine the future with the shells. When he asked her why she wanted so passionately to know about the shells she answered, "Out of love for you, dear Papa, only because I love you."

To this day the only female mediums allowed to throw the cowries are the devotees of Oxum.

OXUMARÊ

If you want to win the lottery you should make an offering to Oxumarê. An Orixá with no Roman Catholic counterpart, Oxumarê is the rainbow, the shining celestial symbol that presages good things, the emblem of prosperity, money, prizes, and happiness. When this deity appears in the sky it is to affirm the continuation of life. Oxumarê makes his presence felt wherever financial negotiations take place, such as banks, the stock exchange, and where bills are paid.

He also presides over financial loss. People invoke the androgynous god's mighty powers when deciding to buy or sell stocks, businesses, dwellings, et cetera.

Oxumarê is also associated with Dã, the cobra of the Voodoo pantheon, but he does not exercise Dã's wide powers. As the sky cobra, Oxumarê arches his body to drink water from the earth, immersing his head and tail in the water to form the rainbow. This entity stands for the hypnotic power of the cobra and the shimmering beauty of the colorful rainbow. In some traditions, Oxumarê is seen as female. The deity's mediums perform a sinuous, contortion-like dance when they incorporate.

Legend

When Oxumarê seduced and enjoyed Oxum, Xangô flew into a terrible rage and killed him. Nanã took pity on the entity and resuscitated him to be Lord of the Stars. Yet in this capacity he was not allowed to touch the ground, which saddened him.

One day Oxalá asked Oxumarê if he knew how to find the most brilliant precious stones on earth.

The Orixá replied, "Of course. Why don't you make an investment with me of 6,000 cowries, and I will take care of you."

"Done!" Oxalá exclaimed and eagerly handed over the shells.

Then Oxumarê told the Orixá to search the seabeds of the world where he would uncover the most beautiful stones on earth. Oxalá discovered impossibly stunning, shimmering gems there. He was so grateful he turned the unhappy Orixá into a snake who could arch his tail and touch both the earth and sky, and thus once again be connected to both worlds.

XANGÔ

When thunder rolls and lightning crackles, the power of Xangô is felt by all. The thunder god is the most respected and cultivated of all the Orixás because he was the first African deity to set foot on Brazilian soil. He represents the "force of the stone" or cosmic justice. The patron of writers, judges, senators, administrators, investigators, monarchs, leaders, and reformers, Xangô symbolizes pure ideology, initiative, decisiveness, the power of the will, the voice of the people.

A proud, fire-breathing, dominating, blue-blooded monarch, he sits aloof on a craggy rock with an open book by his side and a lion at his feet. He causes the volcanos of the earth to erupt in lava flow, expresses the ire of Olórun, and metes out absolute justice to humankind.

Xangô's presence is felt when a person receives an important message by letter, telephone, fax, telex, or telegram. As lawgiver, he presides over courts, ministries, prisons, associations, syndicates, police stations, and all forums. He also inhabits dictionaries, almanacs, encyclopedias, and code books, and he hovers wherever contracts are signed. The only place he does not visit is the realm of the Eguns, because he abhors death. The many concepts this powerful lord represents are so all-encompassing that he has come to be syncretized with several Catholic saints.

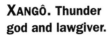

XANGÔ. Thunder god and lawgiver.

Legend

Troops from foreign lands suddenly appeared to make war on the forces of Xangô. Taken aback by their affront, the god retired to his rocky cliff to oversee the battle. He watched while left and right his soldiers were mowed down. The aggressors showed no mercy to the captured troops, slaughtering everyone.

As the carnage continued, Xangô's blood rose until he could no longer contain his wrath. He hammered on his rock, and the sparks ignited by the contact flared up into gigantic lightning bolts that flew to destroy the oppressors. When the divinity's troops, renewed by their leader's vigor, rose up against the foe and conquered them, some of Xangô's officers demanded the right to slaughter them all as vengeance for their comrades' deaths, but Xangô's raised hand stopped them in their tracks.

"The enemy troops are not to blame for the destruction of our men," he pronounced. "They are good soldiers who only followed the orders of their generals, as you do mine. I command you to set them free. We will content ourselves with annihilating their leaders, who are the only ones to blame."

In this way, the people of Xangô, including the pardoned soldiers who now became the Orixá's most loyal followers, learned to temper justice with mercy.

MINOR ORIXÁS

Although the following deities occasionally appear in myths and sometimes are incorporated by mediums, they do not command a wide following in Brazil.

Euá or Ewá

The daughter of Nanã and female twin of Oxumarê (whenever this Orixá is not considered androgynous or female), this lady of the African river by the same name is the goddess of beauty, harmony, and enchantment. She represents all that is fragile and sensitive. Her precinct is the white end of the rainbow. Euá was so beautiful that men would fight to the death to possess her. In order to stop the carnage she changed herself into a puddle of water that evaporated to the sky, condensed into a cloud, and fell as rain. Thus she is known as the deity of transformation. Euá is syncretized with Our Lady of Montserrat.

Iroko

The god Iroko, who is also known as Loko in the Gegê tradition and Time in the Angolan rituals, represents the ever-changing seasons. Time is always in movement because if it stood still, all species would perish. Iroko is syncretized with many saints including Francis of Assisi, Lawrence, and Good Jesus of the Sailors. Interestingly, his visage is represented by the jurema tree, which followers adorn with ribbons, rather like the ancient Celts of northern Europe decorated their sacred trees and wells. Food offerings are also often left at the foot of the trees, especially sacrifices of cock and she-goat. Iroko's dance is performed on the knees with the dancer making movements with his or her hands as if to dig for gold, and then pointing to the sky as if to say, "God is in the sky and also on the earth."

Logun-Odê

This god of fish and fishermen is the son of Oxóssi and Oxum. Sometimes he is portrayed as a female with a stringed musical instrument similar to a lyre with which she enchants all who hear her music. This Orixá's colors are green, blue, and yellow, and he is syncretized with the Archangel Michael. Some legends confuse him with Oxóssi.

Obá

The third wife of Xangô is a warrior goddess syncretized with Joan of Arc. In some legends, Iansã persuades her to cut off her own ear and cook it to please Xangô, while in other stories it is Oxum, who in a fit of jealous rage, lops off her ear with a sword. In any case it is clear, that like Vincent Van Gogh, she loses an ear to love.

While the Orixás are the primary figures in the Afro-Brazilian pantheon, other formidable characters also fill the stage of life and help negotiate humans' destinies on a daily basis. You will meet these powerful entities in the next chapter.

NOTES

1. *Axé* literally means "so be it," but usually refers to the powers of the divinities that are concentrated in the sacred objects of the cult. The sacred objects are then also called *axés*, and they protect, revitalize, and concentrate the energy of the temple's devotees.

2. A *filho-de-santo*, *filha* in the feminine form, is literally a "child of the saint," meaning a cult follower. The cult is considered a family with the leader being a *mãe-de-santo* ("mother of the saint") or a *pai-de-santo* ("father of the saint"). The principal helpers to the mother and father are the "little mother" or "little father." The "sons" and "daughters" are the mediums and worshippers.

3. Other practitioners believe that the older goddess Nanã is the mother of the Orixás.

4. Ifá is the god of destiny and divination, sometimes syncretized with the Holy Ghost. If Exu is the Messenger of Darkness, Ifá is the Bearer of the Light. He is not incorporated in the temple.

CHAPTER 3

FORMIDABLE ENTITIES

The yellow glob of the moon that had begrudgingly lighted our way was now shrouded in a thick curtain of clouds. This, coupled with the fact that the path was overhung by tropical trees weeping with Spanish moss, deprived us of any vestige of natural light and slowed our band's progress even more as we lurched up the tortuous mountain trail. We were also hindered by the voluminous black and red satin capes we wore and the offerings and ritual tools we carried. Someone stumbled and startled an enormous black bird that flapped out of a tree. I could feel its furiously beating wings as it flew by into the darkness screeching a curse at us.

As I peered through the gloom, straining to identify the thousand shapeless masses that I imagined lurking in the shadows watching me, I wondered why I had ever chosen to come out into the wilderness of a tropical forest in the middle of the night with these people. "Primary research," I had to keep telling myself. I had a feline curiosity about what might happen. At last we reached a spot where the trail seemed to bifurcate, slithering off like four snakes from a Medusa's head in different directions. Our leader motioned that we had arrived.

The followers of the Quimbanda Line of Exu silently busied themselves with the preparations. Someone produced a bundle of red and black candles, set them in a large circle in the middle of the crossroads of the five trails, and lighted them. Another participant scratched a profusion of sigils on the ground with black, red, and white chalk pieces called *pembas* (see Chapter 5). Another person filled and placed seven crystal goblets of *cachaça* on the ground. Yet another positioned seven fine cigars in holders all in a neat row, and left a matchbox next to them with seven match heads neatly protruding from the lid.

In the meantime, several cult members set out on the ground a large offering that included components that had been previously determined by throwing the cowrie shells in divination. Since the mystical number of Exu is seven, and we were invoking the influence of the seven Exus, we offered seven of many of the items. Patiently the members of the group arranged the following:

- Red clay from seven different cemeteries.
- Nails and wood chips from seven coffins.
- Bone ash from seven corpses.
- Water from seven beaches, a well, a rainstorm, a waterfall, a brook, a river, a still pool, and a mine shaft.
- Seven different kinds of peppers plus rue and rosemary.
- Black, white, and red pembas.

- Minerals—seven lumps of coal and filings from silver, gold, aluminum, lead, brass, iron, copper, steel, and zinc.

- Twenty-one coins of any value.

- Seven bank notes of any value.

- Animal parts, including an eye of a river dolphin, a snake skin, and a cat's claw.

- Three rolls of parchment.

- Seven cowrie shells.

- Three newspapers printed with the current date.

- A clay image of Exu of the Seven Crossroads complete with a miniature iron trident in his hand and sixteen cowrie shells to accentuate the eyes, nose, teeth, and nails of the statue.

When everything was ready, the leader, accompanied by singing and drumming from the others, intoned a series of invocations, beginning with one to manifest the chief entity, Exu Tranca-Ruas[1]—"Exu Who Locks Up the Streets":

> *Master Tranca-Ruas*
> *It is said that your people belong to the Faith*
> *And we, your devout worshippers say*
> *That your band is the greatest!*
> *Master Tranca-Ruas*
> *We begin the Congo ritual of song and dance*
> *Long live the Faith of Guinea!*[2]
> *Long live the Souls!*[3]
> *Long live the Kingdom of the Faith!*
> *Long live Exu of the Souls!*
> *For he is Tranca-Ruas of the Faith.*
> *Mama is begging the sun*
> *Papa is begging the moon*
> *Your children are begging*
> *The protection of Master Tranca-Ruas!*[4]

Suddenly from out of the darkness, a hulk of a man burst into the circle. The copper-toned skin of his nude torso glistened in the candlelight, and I could distinguish his cloven hoofs and pointed ears.

"*Laroiê!* Welcome *compadre*," everybody greeted him.

The restive entity smiled broadly at his devotees. He quickly bent down, picked up a glass of cachaça and downed it with one gulp. A member of the sect stepped forward and offered him a cigar, then lit it for him.

From another point in the darkness another Exu swaggered into the circle. This one sported a long, black-and-red cape, a shiny top hat, and a waxed mustache. A sardonic smile played on his lips. I half-expected him to let go with a rendition of Mick Jagger's "Sympathy for the Devil"—"Let me introduce myself/I'm a man of wealth and taste...." Instead, he merely leaned over and retrieved his refreshment, then joined the others in the dance that had begun. One by one, the Exus materialized—Bara, Elegbara, Caveira, Marabô, Tiriri[5]—until seven of what to me looked very much like devils cavorted with abandon around us, laughing their loud belly-laughs, puffing greedily on cigars, and swigging sugarcane liquor. We all joined in the saturnalia and felt the pure liberation of our spirits. Surely these were members of the group who had been possessed by Exus, but in the din of the drums and voices, the flickering candles, and general celebration, I could have sworn these entities had emerged from the great, black forest.

The ritual proved to be an all-night affair with much singing, dancing, and partying, but along the way the Exus tendered sound advice to the gathering. As with any religion, all was not peace and light in this terreiro, and the members, most of whom were undergoing both personal and group psychic attack from a rival sect, had in desperation called upon the formidable powers of the Seven Exus to protect them and do battle for them in their hour of need. This was serious business that belied the lighthearted tone of the ritual, and showed the Exus at their most dynamic and masterful.

WHO IS EXU?

Who is Exu and why is he so ardently cultivated in Brazilian magick? Ask ten Brazilians—regardless of whether or not they are followers of African traditions. They will all know about him, and will probably give you ten different answers.[6]

Some will tell you that Exu works black magick; others will say that he undoes evil spells. Still other people will refer to him not as an Orixá, but as a messenger, a kind of Mercury-Hermes-Thoth figure— the "Great Communicator" of Afro-Brazilian myth. Then there are the believers who call Exu the universal agent of magick. All of these interpretations are correct. Exu represents a concept so broad and deep that the entire Afro-Brazilian magickal belief system unfolds from it.

Exu is the paradigm of equilibrium. He represents the axis of stability between humans and their gods. Yet since the idea of balance implies equilibrium, he is constantly on the move. One can liken him to a runner on a rocky road—always in danger of falling, but completely steady at the point where both feet leave the ground and fly through the air.

Exu does everything backwards, which is why his children often ask him to do the opposite of what they desire. By acting in reverse, he teaches that blind obedience to authority or the established order of things is wrong, and that ritual often obscures meaning. He reminds his followers that they should be prepared to re-interpret reality from a fresh point of view so the situation does not stagnate. It is no wonder that those who work with Exu's energy have a tricky time of it.

TWO REPRESENTATIONS OF EXU. *Left:* **Exu Gira-Mundo (World Spinner).** *Right:* **Exu Casamenteiro (Marrying Exu).**

Many perceive Exu as a prankster, always trying to throw a person off pace. He toys with human sensibilities and upsets the status quo because he represents the necessary power of disorder that must occasionally occur for one to be able to rebuild on more solid ground. In this sense, he can be compared to the Tower trump in the tarot.

A Portuguese expression that cogently defines this thought is *grau de sandice*, "grain of insanity." Exu represents the kernel of madness that sparks all creativity. He embodies physical, mental, and spiritual fertility because he typifies the creative impulse. Thus he is often depicted naked with sexual organ exposed and aroused.

Mário César Barcellos, a Candomblé initiate and writer in the field, sums up well the importance of this entity to human life when he says that "Exu represents our inner selves, he is the most intimate part of our being, our power to be good or evil in accordance with our individual wills. Exu is the most obscure point deeply hidden within a human being, and at the same time he is what is most obvious and clear."[7]

**EXU DAS SETE ENCRUZILHADAS.
(Exu of the Seven Crossroads.)**

If the truth be told, people are reticent to face their inner selves, afraid to reinterpret reality, experience the exigencies of the Tower trump. Human nature is resistant to change and everything else that Exu represents. This is why some depict him as a devil, and dress him up in horns, hooves, and tail.

Before any ceremony (such as the one that begins this chapter) takes place, cult members will make a sacrificial offering to Exu and to the "People of the Street," as his minions are called. This is partly so that he will deliver their petitions to the Orixás, but also so that he will not do anything to disturb the proceedings. Many people do not like surprises, and may recoil from a situation that they think they cannot handle. But Exu is quite insistent; he is always there to upset the boat because he challenges people to expand their horizons—or not—as they wish.

Barcellos tells a story about Exu that typifies the way he acts (the story is paraphrased here).[8] One day Exu was wandering around the countryside and spied a fertile bit of farmland that he took a hankering to possess. He noticed that it was partitioned off down the middle by a fence, and through inquiries, discovered that the plots belonged to two friends. He offered the owners a generous amount for the land, but they refused to sell.

Undaunted, the trickster devised a plan. He took a cap that he painted white on one side and red on the other, threw it down on the property line, and waited behind a bush.

As was their custom, the two friends came by on their daily walk to survey their lands. At the same time they both spied the cap. One friend said to the other, "What's a red cap doing on my property?"

The other replied, "It's not a red cap. It's a white cap, and it's on my property."

An argument ensued that escalated until they grabbed their hoes and bludgeoned each other to death.

Exu, who witnessed the carnage from his hiding place, shuffled over and picked up the cap from the ground. As he turned away, he commented, "But what confused beings these humans are anyway! They can't even manage to solve the simplest of problems!" Through their own mean natures, prodded into action by Exu's intervention, the farmers had managed to do themselves in.

The Quimbandists, rather than sacrifice to Exu out of fear and live in hope that he will leave them alone, joyfully embrace this entity as the symbol of freedom from oppression. For the Quimbandist, the Exus (and hundreds of them exist) represent the heroes of the quilombo of Palmares,[9] where Black and Indian slaves escaped from the servitude of the plantation and fought side-by-side to establish their own free state in the forest. For them, Exu is the spirit that fomented resurrection in the slave quarters and fought for liberty in the jungle. He is also the spirit of wild, unabashed free love, all of which is symbolized by his and his female counterparts', the Pombas-Giras, blatantly sexual attire, suggestive mannerisms, and unbridled desires. When the Quimbandist makes an offering to Exu, it is to open

EXAMPLES OF POMBAS-GIRAS. *Left to right:* **Pomba-Gira Cigna (Gypsy), Pomba-Gira Sete Encruzilhadas (Seven Crossroads), Pomba-Gira Maria Padiha (Mary Little Sandalfoot).**

wide the doors to communication between the natural and the supernatural worlds in every possible way.

Those who view Exu as an inferior, unevolved entity maintain that he is the servant of the deities and that each Orixá possesses an Exu who, like a slave, does its bidding. In this system, both "baptized" and "pagan" Exus populate the supernatural universe. Baptized Exus, it is supposed, realize that they are not evolved, and try to improve themselves by protecting humans from harm, and by performing only good under the orientation of a human guide. One source explains their use to humans by likening them to "policemen who penetrate the marginal regions of the universe, attracting malefic beings to their legions so they can arrest and instruct them."[10]

On the other hand, the pagan Exus know they are without redemption, so do not hesitate to perform the most repulsive and condemnable acts. They suffer and continue to cause suffering in a vicious cycle of hatred and obsession until one day, it is hoped, they will be awakened to the self-defeating nature of their behavior.

One reason the ritual that begins this chapter took place at a crossroads is because that is there Exu dwells. The crossroads symbolizes the entity as the Great Communicator and expander of horizons. In Exu's precinct things happen, people and ideas meet, pass, and are exchanged. At a crossroads, spaces open up and close down, and new directions are taken. In this sense, Exu rules the intelligence and stands for sagacity and wisdom. Deep down, his home is the ground. He guards the sacred, fathomless well of knowledge, and as such, is often likened to Saint Peter.

Because of his omniscience, Exu is privy to the mysteries of life and death. Thus he also presides over the cowrie shell divination game that charts the fates of humankind. The three-pronged trident he carries symbolizes the past, present, and future or positive, negative, and neutral in accordance with the orientation of the believer.

Exu is also linked with Omulu and Ogum because he is familiar with all life's secrets, including those of pestilence, disease, and death, and how to make and use weapons (which are often the agents of death).

In a broader sense than the way those who fear him visualize, his role is that of the interlocutor of the gods, because, though he may associate with them, he is not one of them. Each Orixá works within a specific domain, but Exu is at home in all their abodes and moves freely among them. Expressed from another point of view, each Orixá embodies one or another of Exu's characteristics, but none is wholly like him. Exu is honored because without his essence the Orixás could not manifest their powers. He receives the very first sacrifices in any ritual, and is "dispatched" at the end of the session so that he may carry the petitions of the congregation to the Orixás.

Not because he is an unevolved entity, but because of his unique nature, Exu cannot be equated with an Orixá. Whatever he represents to you depends on your personal interpretation. If you believe him to be an agent of evil and destruction, he will rise to the occasion. If you think he is good, he will behave benevolently—probably. (Remember, his nature is unpredictable!) If you see him as a neutral agent, again this chameleon will satisfy your expectations. Whatever Exu or Pomba-Gira really means is very much up to you.

BRAZILIAN HISTORICAL FIGURES
Pretos Velhos

Father Cândido, missionary spirit among us, we beg
you, Father, not to abandon us even for a moment,
and especially to attend us during the critical
moments of our lives. Help us to find the path of love
and charity, give us the power and will to bear the
heavy load of the path to Zambi that we have cho-
sen. Give us health, peace, and happiness in accor-
dance to our merit.[11]

Arguably the most popular entities in the Brazilian pantheon, the Pretos Velhos,[12] one of which is Father Cândido mentioned above, represent the spirits of Black slaves who in past centuries suffered hard lives toiling for their White masters. Brazilians conceive of them as people who once lead terrestrial lives. Through their ordeals they developed the virtues of humility and kindness, and learned about folk medicine in order to heal the ailing. Now they have become elevated spirits who return to earth out of their profound sympathy for humanity.

The spirits of Pretos Velhos manifest through the bodies of mediums. When called upon in invocations like the prayer cited above, the spirits themselves humbly ask permission of the terreiro members to enter the sacred space. There they share their secrets, known as *mandingas*, in order to heal suffering, practice charity, and console those who have been physically or emotionally wounded. It is believed that these sages are not always spirits of slaves; sometimes they may actually be former slave masters who are returning to earth to expiate past sins through their impersonations. Other times, it is suspected that they represent highly evolved entities who incorporate in the form of an old Black slave in order to communicate the fruits of their knowledge in more humanly apprehensible terms.

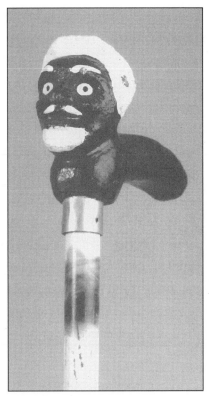

PRETOS VELHOS. *Left:* Mãe Benedita ("Blessed Mother") Preta Velha smoking a traditional pipe. Note her simple white costume and beads. *Right:* A Preto Velho (spirit of an old Black slave), pictured with a cane to lean on while incorporated.

The Pretos Velhos speak in a simple language, but often in an antiquated Portuguese dialect that is difficult to understand. This is why an *Ekêde* (whom you will meet in Chapter 4) sits by the incorporated entity with pen and paper in hand during consultations. She interprets the entity's speech for the client and writes down the recipes for better health that the spirit may offer.

After a Preto Velho incorporates, the medium is escorted to the dressing room to be clothed in the style of the entity. That style often consists of a plain white skirt or pair of pants; bare chest or a simple shirt or blouse; a beard (if the spirit is a male); a pipe full of fragrant tobacco; and a cane to lean on. The Preto Velho slowly returns to the main salon and squats on the floor or on a low, three-legged stool. The client then kneels or stoops to hear the proffered words of advice.

The entities may propose simple remedies culled from folk medicine, or will perform psychic readings like the one at the beginning of Chapter 6. They may simply give good counsel, or more rarely, convey complex concepts through symbolic language. They may also help rid the body of negative fluids that are believed to impede spiritual development, or help people understand the reasons behind life's trials and tribulations and the inexorability of the wills of the gods. They inspire mediums to nurture their psychic abilities, always in the same soft, soothing tones of encouragement. Every act they perform is done in the spirit of human charity and with immense love.

The Caboclos

A Song to Sing ▲	*Our Lady has censed her altar*
While Censing	*For her blessed son to smell.*
the Sacred Space	*I cense my Caboclo village*
for the Advent	*So evil will flee and good will enter in.*
of the Caboclos	*I am censing*
	I am fumigating
	The home of my god.
	Cense, censer
	Cense the house of my forefathers. [14]

Unlike the Pretos Velhos who learned their wise ways through humility and suffering, the Caboclos, half-breed Indians, inhabit the celestial realms because they risked their lives to save the Brazilian people. They battled the overlords and won independence for Brazil. It is said that Caboclos fought side-by-side as comrades with the Blacks in renegade colonies such as Palmares. Thus, they were idealized for their independence, nobility of spirit, courage, and vast knowledge of the forest. (I say idealized, because if one were to be absolutely truthful, most Indians were either wiped out or ran away into the forest. After all, it is the myth, not historical accuracy, that counts in the cosmogony of the Afro-Brazilian system.)[15] Although they do not behave in a soft-spoken and mild manner like the Pretos Velhos, these proud entities are ready, willing, and able to act with alacrity and precision to reverse injustices, practice charity, and benefit humanity.

THE CABOCLOS. *Left:* Caboclo Treme-Terra (Earth Shaker). *Right:* Caboclo Sete Demandas (Seven Demands). One could call upon either of these Caboclos when seeking redress from an injustice.

Here is a typical story about the life of a Caboclo. Once in the middle of the last century there was a half-breed cowboy who worked for a wealthy rancher in the *sertão*, the dry lands of the northeast. Guaicuru was a dextrous cowhand, renowned for his skill with a lariat and unbeatable at rounding up cattle and sheep. His only downfall was that demon, firewater.

Once, when out looking for a lost calf, he overindulged, and fell asleep at the foot of a mango tree. A passing ocelot discovered and devoured him. Cut down in the prime of life, he yearned for more time on earth. So he returned to repent his vice, do good, and chase the Eguns (the spirits of the dead) from everyone's path with his cracking whip.

Seven legions of Caboclos[16] work in the line of Oxóssi. These, plus the Caboclos of the lines of Ogum and Xangô, constitute the pyramidical concentration of energy for the rites of Umbanda that involve constructing and casting spells. In other words, the Caboclos who work the wills of these remarkable Orixás form the supreme force of Umbanda.

The faithful greet the Caboclos with this salutation from an unknown Indian language, *Okê bambi ô crinó!* With this greeting the entities descend into the terreiro, their bronzed bodies clad in trousers rolled up to the knee, red sashes crossed and tied over deeply tanned chests, bodies and clothing bejeweled with green and white feathers and white stones. They brandish wooden or stone representations of coral snakes. The Caboclos' manner may be difficult to deal with at first because they seem haughty, independent, and initially uncommunicative. This is because they symbolize the freedom of the sun, the moon, and the wind. If the petitioner is patient and placates his whims the Caboclo will always provide the right solution to any problem, and will act tirelessly to awaken any child of the gods to his or her fullest potential.

Songs to the Caboclos

The four songs translated below are sung in the places of worship and show the strong, independent character of the Caboclo. They are meant either to invoke the Indians to descend into the temple or celebrate their many virtues.

Caboclo of the **White Feather**	▲	*Our Caboclos live in your village,* *The waterfalls flow through your forest.* *A golden feather sparkles on your kilt* *Your helmet glitters on the dawn.*[17]
Caboclo **Trail-Blazer**	▲	*I am Caboclo Trail-Blazer* *I am bound to settle all disputes* *When Caboclo Trail-Blazer is called upon* *No case can be lost.*[18]
Caboclo **Redskin**	▲	*We are the Caboclos of the red skin.* *Toss up the waves,* *For the moonlight is illuminating the night!*[19]
Waterfall **Caboclo**	▲	*The water flows from the mountains* *Descending through the grotto* *Beating the stones* *It is a waterfall* *In the Temple of Umbanda* *They are arriving* *Waterfall Caboclo's band.*[20]

Cabocla Jurema

Famous female Caboclas[21] also inhabit the legends of the Umbanda, Catimbó, and Batuque[22] sects, but none are as ardently cultivated as Cabocla Jurema. The Lady of the Forest is revered for her vast knowledge of herbal medicine and for the ardor with which she flies to the aid of the weak and infirm. She is associated with Ossãe, the potent herbal divinity (see Chapter 2) and represents the female counterpart of this god.

Her sacred tree, the *Pithecolobium tortum*, is called by her own name in the vernacular. An entire cult of followers has evolved around Jurema's tree because the root, bark, and fruit of this tree is a powerful hallucinogen. Followers of the Jurema cult, known as *Juremados*, are initiated in a ceremony called a *juremação*, in which the aspirant drinks the juice and falls into a trance. An incision is made in the body where a tiny amulet is introduced; it forever marks, links, and protects the believer by the power of Jurema. Jurema's children believe that after imbibing the juice in ritual, their spirits can leave their bodies and travel astrally to other villages to cure the afflicted.

Offerings left to Jurema at the foot of her tree include the herb *guaraná*, honey, candles, perfume, holy water, vials of mercury, *dendê* oil, cachaça, wine, champagne, bows and arrows, and painted hides. Other trees of the same genus are also sacred to Jurema;

Cabocla Jurema.

these include the white jurema (*P. diversifoium*) and the black jurema (*Mimosa nigra*).

The following are some invocations to Jurema:

Invocations
to Jurema

▲ *When I was seven months old*
My mother abandoned me.
Hail to the name of Oxóssi!
It was a Tupi[23] *Indian who raised me!*
O Jurema's companions, hear me,
I am in pain!
Poor me, my companions!
Poor me so all alone![24]

▲ *Jurema left her forests*
She came to dance in this kingdom.
Oh look, a child of Jurema,
Welcoming her!
Iara, the mermaid of the sea!
Jurema left her forests
She comes to dance in this kingdom!
Oh look at the child of Jurema
Performing a curimba[25]
On the edge of the sea![26]

Spirits of Orientals

Although one can see why the Pretos Velhos and Caboclos who originate in Brazilian history were revivified by the popular Brazilian religions, it is perhaps more difficult to understand these sects' Oriental connection. As indicated in Chapter 1, one of the commandments of the Law of Umbanda exhorts adherents to respect all religions. This affirmation underscores the strong universalist thread that runs through the Afro-Brazilian belief system. Umbandists set great store by

Oriental philosophy because they believe that the East is the cradle of all religions and philosophies. For example, early Umbandist doctrine was strongly influenced by Theosophy,[27] which is based on Eastern traditions.

In order to bring the wisdom of the Orient to the terreiro, Umbandists call upon the spirits of magi to enter the bodies of their mediums. On "Oriental Night," as it is called, the drums are silenced, the temple is assiduously purified with incense, and myriads of white candles are lighted. The mediums, who have not had sexual relations, smoked, or drunk liquor for twenty-four hours prior to the ceremony, take a purification bath and dress entirely in white. Then they meditate on their high purpose silently in the lightly perfumed environment. Soon the spirit guides softly descend and impart their profound wisdom. Their presence is received with gratitude because the believers know that unlike some entities, the Oriental magi are not obliged to come down to earth, and only do so out of a spirit of immense love for humanity and a desire to help those in need.

EGUNS

The Eguns are spirits of the dead, sometimes unenlightened souls, other times, souls of revered ancestors who return to earth from time to time in certain ceremonies. The only Orixá who can dominate these spirits is Iansã, who does not fear them.

In order to set the mood for understanding what happens during some of the rites for the dead, the following is a translation and paraphrase of a description of a funeral ritual.

Notes from an Axexê Rite Celebrated on the First Anniversary of the Death of an Ialorixá

> We arrived around 9:00 P.M. after having climbed a fairly steep road bordered by banana trees and yellow and blue painted cottages. ...(The researchers entered the main salon of the terreiro and noticed) some objects covered by a white towel and a kind of throne that was little more than a small platform suspended between two white walls. It was here where the *mãe-de-santo* had sat on ceremonial occasions. Now a large framed photograph of her hung on the wall behind the throne. The *terreiro*, which had a central post, was illuminated by neon lights.

The author says that all the female devotees, who sat on mats against one wall, were dressed in white with matching, flowing shawls. The audience, largely consisting of young men, were ensconced on benches pushed up against the opposite wall. Even though ritual chanting and dancing were going on, no one seemed to pay much attention. They laughed and talked among themselves.

The author and his companion, Pierre Verger, the famous Candomblé researcher, were led over to be introduced to the future mãe-de-santo, for it was the funeral of a terreiro chief that the men were witnessing. The new leader was a very small, ancient Black woman with a round face and full jowls. She did not seem particularily pleased to see the intruders.

> Suddenly the group went quiet. Everybody stood and began to clap when the two men with slow and respectful gestures raised the towel (from the platform). Beneath it were two large, painted jars, a bottle, a pouch, a bag, a pile of ashes, a plate, and some fans fashioned from palm fronds. Then they took away the other cloth that covered a bottle gourd that was tipped upside down in a plate full of water.

The two men then seated themselves on little benches behind the jars, and began to fold up the fans (which they had uncovered). The one behind the gourd held two little sticks in his hands.

At this point in the proceedings, the new mãe-de-santo assumed command and began to wail a Gegê lament.

The musicians accompanied her by tapping the mouths of the jugs with the fans, producing a hollow sound like playing a drum, only more muffled. Sometimes they changed the timbre by resting their left hands on the fans when they tapped the mouths of the jugs. The third musician thumped on the bottle gourd. The *mãe-de-santo* and her assistant moved in front of the musicians and each took a fistful of ashes, which they threw at the spectators. Then they began to dance on the same spot with their arms extended in front of them and the palms of their hands open. The filhas-de-santo followed by the members of the audience, came one by one, and deposited little cent pieces in their hands. Soon the dancers held an abundant supply in their cupped hands. At the end of the dance the two women deposited the money on the plate.[29]

The above story describes the beginning of an *axexê* ritual for the dead in a Candomblé terreiro in Bahia. Although the privacy of these rituals is a closely guarded secret, and details differ from sect to sect and terreiro to terreiro, certain common patterns emerge.

Usually cult members and close family of the deceased attend by invitation. The purpose of the ritual is to honor the dead and to send the spirit off into the universe so it does not become an Egun, a discarnate soul that keeps returning to earth. Sacrifices are made to the soul of the dead person, and the individual's material effects are packed up in a bundle and dispatched with ceremony into a body of water.

The drums, which normally are played to call down the spirits, remain covered "in mourning" for a time because otherwise they might entice the Eguns to descend. Although there is singing and dancing, other instruments, such as bells and gourds, mark the rhythm instead.

At one point during the ceremony, the head Orixá of the deceased is called upon to descend to earth in order to make the spirit realize that its medium (or "horse," as the medium is sometimes called) has passed away, and that the Orixá must now find another vehicle for its manifestation. The Orixá may "ride another horse," take possession of another medium for a while, until it realizes that it must return to its heavenly abode.

Great care is taken at the end of the rite to chase away any Eguns who may have lingered. Even those who attend the beginning of the ritual are made to stay until the final dispatching ceremony at the end, so that no Egun may attach itself like a succubus to an unsuspecting member of the sect or audience and remain in this mundane place. Participants generally bind a bracelet called a *contra-Egun*, fashioned from braided herbs and straw, tightly to their arms to further protect them from the soul of the dead person and other Eguns.

The number of days a ceremony continues varies according to the grade the deceased attained in the terreiro. For example, a rite for the death of a spiritual leader may last for seven days; it can be repeated after one year and again after seven years. Sometimes, the terreiro remains sealed for an entire year. No rituals take place, and the chosen leader cannot take command until at least the one-year ceremony has been completed.

The ritual described above may take place in the center of the terreiro, or if the temple is rich enough, the congregation may set aside a separate house for the Eguns called a *balê*. In this case, the ritual is celebrated outside the house and the deceased's effects are gathered into a bundle called a *carrego* and deposited inside by members who worship on the Line of the Souls. The house of the Eguns is a little cubicle similar to the one provided for Exu, except it is topped by a cross. Inside receptacles hold food such as roasted cock and popcorn for the Eguns. On the altar lay broken bits of china as a symbol of the life that has departed. If the temple does not have a balê, the carrego is dispatched in a river or the sea. The effects of the deceased leader include both personal items and any assentamentos, magickal fetishes that the leader had prepared for the terreiro. In this way, the temple is cleared of the leader's influence, and a new chief can by chosen from the deceased's testament or by throwing the cowrie shells.

In the above ritual, the members all dressed in white, which is the Afro-Brazilian color of death. Not mentioned in the description is the fact that sometimes an officer known as the *Ogê* or *Anixa* will carry a black-and-white striped stick called the *ixá*, which he holds out in front of him to contain the Eguns.

Cultivating the Eguns

God works with God,
The Souls work in the sea.
He who takes a pemba in hand is persistent.
With the Souls one should never be obstinate. [30]

At this point, you may be asking yourself why anybody would want to worship the Eguns. The answer to this question, like everything involved in the Afro-Brazilian religions, is complex and subject to subtle interpretation.

It is believed that the soul represents a person's intelligence and that it protects the individual's emotional nature after death. After the body dies, the soul may not be convinced of its new state, and therefore harnesses emotions to react negatively to the situation. It takes possession of live human bodies, causing disturbances that can vary from something as innocuous as playing tricks or giving false advice to something as serious as causing harm to the medium's physical or psychic body. The emotional being can even interfere with the descent of an Orixá into a human vehicle. Therefore, the souls, or Eguns, are sometimes feared and shooed away from the terreiro.

On the other hand, many wise and generous spirits from the glorious spheres of infinity can materialize on the Umbanda Line of the Souls to render sound counsel and open the human spirit to the path of the higher. These spirits are called *Babás*, and they are cultivated at separate *pejis*, or at a little house with an altar called *Ikê Ibó Ibú*.

At this altar, white manioc flour, liquor with bee honey, and other delicacies meant for their refreshment await the descent of these august entities. When mediums incorporate Egun spirits, they don rich fabric costumes decorated with beads, leather, little mirrors, and a hood known as a *filá*, and carry a whip. The Eguns choreograph a richly complicated dance and speak with cavernous voices. The rites are steeped in mystery and tradition, but the followers of the Eguns claim that the complicated ceremonial procedures are worth the trouble.

The term *Egun* comes from a Yoruba word that means "bone" or "skeleton." Officers of the sect include the *Alibá*, chief of the *Ojés*, priests of the sect who are the most involved in the rituals. The *Edun* is a follower who cares for and makes sure nobody enters the *peji* or terreiro where worship takes place. The *Majebajó* directs most of the rituals.

▲ ▲ ▲

Now that you have learned about the formidable entities of the Afro-Brazilian pantheon, the next chapter will introduce you to the human beings who dare work with their power.

NOTES

1. Exu Tranca-Ruas is the great guardian Exu who represents all the Orixás, and in Esoteric Umbanda works in the Line of Ogum. This means that he protects terreiros and all participants. His name means "He Who Locks up the Streets."

2. In centuries gone by, the name "Guinea" referred to the entire west coast of Africa from the mouth of the Senegal River to the mouth of the Congo. Although contemporary Guinea covers a much smaller area, members of Afro-Brazilian sects still use the term in an almost romantic sense to refer to the land of their forefathers, the land of milk and honey from whence their gods and their religion came.

3. *As Almas*, "the Souls," is another name for the souls of the dead who work under Tranca-Ruas.

4. Decelso (Celso Rosa), *Babalâos e Ialorixás*, 2nd ed. (Rio de Janeiro, Editora Eco, n.d.), 95.

5. There is a myriad of Exus with inventive names and even more inventive occupations. Some of the more famous include Elegbara (Power Master), Brasa (Hot Coal), Caveira (Prince of the Cemetery), Cheiroso (Fragrant), Capa Preta (Black Cape), Cobra Coral (Coral Snake), Mangueira (Mango Tree), Sete Encruzilhadas (Seven Crossroads), Gira-Mundo (World Spinner), Marabô (Protector), Arranca-Toco (Destroyer of Obstacles), Meia-Noite (Midnight), Sete Catacumbas (Seven Catacombs), Tiriri (Great Merit), and Veludo (Hide-Covered).

6. Much of this description is rephrased from the introduction I wrote to a translation of the book *Pomba-Gira: The Formidable Female Messenger of the Gods* by Antonio Teixeira Alves Neto (Burbank, CA, Technicians of the Sacred, 1990). This book goes into greater detail about the female Exus than can be expressed here.

7. Mário César Barcellos, *Os Orixás e o Segredo da Vida: Lógica, Mitologia e Ecologia* (Rio de Janeiro: Editora Pallas), 51.

8. Ibid., 49–50.

9. A *quilombo* is a settlement of runaway slaves, and Palmares, which was founded in the interior of the state of Alagoas, was the largest (20,000 inhabitants) and most long-lived (1672–1694) of these establishments. Throughout the Colonial era, slaves were brought to Brazil, very much as they were brought to the South of the U.S. to work the land, especially the sugar plantations. Many slaves escaped and formed their own jungle colonies, which were organized according to the African model, and which became quasi-independent,

pseudo-African states. The quilombos were eventually destroyed by government troops, but they live on in the popular imagination.

10. Vera Braga de Souza Gomes, O *Ritual da Umbanda: Fundamentos Esotéricos* (Rio de Janeiro: Editora Technoprint, 1989), 109.

11. Pompílio de Eufrázio, *Catecismo do Umbandista* (Rio de Janeiro: Editora Eco, 1974), 138–139.

12. Literally the words *preto velho* mean "old Black man" or "woman." During Colonial times, many slaves earned a degree of respect and even love from the general population. Often the women were nannies to the White children on the plantation, and both African men and women knew a great deal about herbal medicine. This was an important skill during a time when doctors were scarce in cities and virtually non-existent in the country. Priests were also in short supply, so the Catholics tended to pay more serious attention than they normally might to African Candomblés that went on in the slave quarters. This respect for African traditions is one reason the religion has persisted into modern times, and also a reason so much faith continues to be put in the folk remedies recommended by the Pretos Velhos.

13. The term *caboclo* means "copper-hued," and refers to the dark color of the skin of these mixed breed Indian-Caucasians. Indians were enslaved as were the Blacks, but being hunters and gatherers, they were of too independent a spirit to stay in the White settlements.

14. José Ribeiro, *Comidas de Santos e Oferendas*, 2nd ed. (Rio de Janeiro: Editora Eco, n.d.), 83.

15. As occurred in the U.S. and Europe, Brazilians of the last century romanticized the Indian. The natives represented the "noble savage" who was pure of heart and unsullied by civilization. Romantic novels of the time by authors such as José de Alencar (*O Guaraní, Iracema*, et cetera) glorified the Indian, as these novels are still read by Brazilian school children. Today, the new Romantics—the environmentalists—are such persistent advocates of Indian rights that the myth of the noble savage still survives in the popular imagination. This is one reason many Brazilians give their children Indian names such as Moema, Bartira, and Uytán.

16. Although the number of Caboclos is almost infinite, the most famous are: Araribóia, chief of the Line of Oxóssi and historical chief of an Indian tribe, who is said in Colonial times to have fought alongside the Portuguese to oust the French invaders from Rio de Janeiro; Arranca-Toco (Driver Away of Difficulties); Arruda (Rue), in reference to the magickal powers of this plant; Cobra Coral (Coral Snake); Pedra Branca (White Stone); Sol e Lua (Sun and Moon);

Vento (Wind); Guiné (Guinea), a region of Africa and a plant by the same name; Malembá (God of Procreation), who represents Oxalá; Pena Branca (White Feather); Sete Encruzilhadas (Seven Crossroads); Treme-Terra (Earthquake).

17. Decelso (Celso Rosa), *Umbanda de Caboclos*, 3rd ed. (Rio de Janeiro: Editora Eco, 1967), 136.

18. Ibid., 142.

19. Ibid., 144.

20. Ibid., 143–144.

21. Well-known Caboclas include Estrela do Mar (Star of the Sea), Inhassã (represents Iansã on the Line of Iemanjá), Iara (Cabocla of the Rivers, also known as Mother of the Waters), Nanã Burucurim (represents Nanã and the Undines), and Sereia do Mar (Mermaid of the Sea, another of Iemanjá's Caboclas).

22. *Batuques* are Afro-Brazilian cults of the southernmost state of Rio Grande do Sul. It is also a term used for some Nagô and Pajelança sects. The word properly refers to certain African dances.

23. The Tupi are a native Brazilian tribe. The term also refers to their language.

24. Antonio Teixeira Alves Neto, *Oxóssi*, 2nd ed. (Rio de Janeiro, Editora Eco, 1967), 58.

25. *Curimba*, also spelled *Corimba*, refers to ritual songs that honor the deities.

26. Decelso, *Umbanda de Caboclos*, 121.

27. "Theosophy" refers to several mystical and esoteric systems that show the relationship of humans to god and the universe. The most famous Theosophist, Madame Helena Petrovna Blavatsky (1831–1891), a Russian mystic, founded the famous Theosophical Society in 1875.

28. Pierre Verger is a well-known researcher and writer about Candomblé sects. Some of his writings are listed in the bibliography.

29. In Jorge Alberto Varanda, *Os Eguns do Candomble* (Rio de Janeiro: Editora Eco, n.d.), 88–90. The description Varanda quotes is by Alfredo Metraux.

30. Decelso, *Babalâos e Ialorixás*, 74.

CHAPTER 4

BELIEVERS AND THEIR SACRED GROUND

The first night I saw her, she reposed in august splendor on a red velvet throne, attended by her entourage. She wore a short skirt made from red and white squares over leggings of the same pattern. Two white sashes crossed in back and fell over her breasts. These were held in place by another red sash. A blazing jewelled tiara crowned her head, and on her arms shimmered red-and-white and copper bracelets and armbands. A double-bladed copper ax flashed in her hand, and on the ax head her glowing fetish was tied in miniature along with her *otá*, a black, sacred stone. This was no slim, agile woman sitting in the chair, but the male Orixá

Xangô Agodá, the mighty thunder god, also known as Saint Gerome, the lawgiver. He had taken possession of the body of Dona Nilsa, the renowned Ialorixá[1] of the Umbandist Temple of Xangô Agodá.

Even if I had been allowed, I dared not approach this imposing figure while she was in trance. Instead, I worked up the courage to return later in the week to ask my questions about the organization and hierarchy of her terreiro. I found Dona Nilsa, when not possessed by her saint, to be a a lively, well-spoken, intelligent woman with a delightful sense of humor. She told me that in her day job she worked as a dietician in a private clinic, joking that during the day she looked after patients' physical bodies, and at night, she cared for their spiritual selves. She took the time out of her busy schedule to instruct me about the inner workings of terreiros, which at the time were very confusing to me.

SPIRITUAL LEADERS: BABALORIXÁS AND IALORIXÁS

The temples of the Afro-Brazilian faiths, which are often known as terreiros, are tightly structured operating units because, according to Dona Nilsa and others, this is the best way to create, nurture, and consolidate the group's axé. The timing and completion of tasks, division of labor, and parceling out of responsibilities that produce the spiritual strength of the organization are all carried out under the direct orders of the temple's reigning Orixá.

In Umbanda, it is the chief Orixá for whom the center is named and who takes possession of the spiritual leader that rules the roost—not the terrestrial leader, as it may appear to the outsider. Nonetheless, critics complain that spiritual leaders hold a frightening amount of personal power over their parishioners. Terreiro chiefs counter that hand-in-hand with this influence comes a serious responsibility. The leader represents the point of equilibrium of the terreiro. He or she must constantly check the physical, mental, psychic, and spiritual barometer of the sacred space and its inhabitants, and be prepared to take quick action if a crack in the structure of the axé is sensed. Any disequilibrium will lead to the ebbing away of the magickal force. This can be exhausting work, fitting only for the most energetic and dedicated filho-de-santo (child of the gods), as a cult follower is called.

In ancient Africa, only males could become leaders, but when the religion was transported to Brazil, women were the ones who kept the ancient faith alive. Priestesses of Xangô from the royal palace of Oyó in Africa formed the first terreiros in the Bahian region of Brazil, and from then on, were accepted equally as leaders. The only privilege an Ialorixá does not enjoy as female leader is permission to divine using the Ifá game (see Chapter 5). Although this task is still reserved exclusively for Babalorixás,[2] the male leaders, the Ialorixás are allowed to divine with cowrie shells.

At first, spiritual chiefs were chosen among Black slaves or their descendants, and leadership was passed down from generation to generation. As these religions spread through the populace, the race of the leader and the practitioners themselves were no longer seen as important. Nowadays in many centers, the chief prepares a testament with a list of filhos-de-santo, which carefully delineates the line of succession. Whoever takes over when a leader dies depends almost entirely on skills and attributes, not family ties. Usually the successor is the the leader's principal assistant.

Babalorixás or Ialorixás must serve at least seven years as an initiate in their own terreiros before being considered as a candidate for a leadership position. They preside over public and private ceremonies, initiations, and sacrifices; prepare the Orixás' assentamentos;[3] act as counselors, spiritual mentors, and educators; and administer methods

for the smooth running of the terreiro. They resolve questions and disputes, tell fortunes by divination, punish infractions, and sometimes
collect and prepare botanicals for medicinal and ritual purposes.

In return, all the head Orixás of all the filhos serve the leader's head
Orixá, who, as mentioned, controls the terreiro. In other words, the
Orixás, or divinities, are perceived as the actual directors of the establishment, and the human practitioners, including the spiritual leader,
merely follow their orders.

Many terreiros, particularly in Candomblé traditions, adhere to an
autocratic structure with specific duties parsed out among various
members. Each person is instructed and knows very well where his or
her responsibilities lie. Woe be unto the one who does not comply; it is
believed that any break in the ritual structure will upset the equilibrium of the temple's axé.

PRINCIPAL OFFICERS
Babá-Kekerê or Iá-Kekerê

The subchief and principal assistant to the spiritual leader (and usually this person's successor), the *Babá-Kekerê* (male) or *Iá-Kekerê*
(female)[4] presides over rituals when the leader is away, ill, or in a
trance. This person rings the *adjá* (a kind of bell, see Appendix E) in the
ear of the Iaô to assist the medium in attaining a trance state, and
directs the Iaôs in their dances. This person also attends to the mediums' education, personal hygiene,[5] and other necessities. The Kekerês,
besides having at least seven years initiation under their sashes, so to
speak, set an example of tranquility, humility, understanding, knowledge, and experience for others to emulate. In other words, the Kekerê
is like a rock that others cling to for stability. These pivotal players have
their own assistants to help them with running the temple.

THE ADJÁ. A bell instrument sounded in the medium's ear to help facilitate a trance.

Ialaxé

Often the third most eminent member of the spiritual hierarchy is the *Ialaxé*,[6] a female initiate with at least seven years' initiation. She cares for the sacred stones, plants, metals, and foods of the Orixás, and keeps the altars clean. This woman enjoys the complete confidence of the male spiritual leader. However, a female chief does not rely on the assistance of an Ialaxé, but carries out these duties on her own.

Cambono

Another dominant figure of the hierarchy is the *Cambone*,[7] the male or female who assists the leader and other mediums when they are incorporated (that is, whenever they are in a trance and the Orixás have taken possession of their bodies). This auxiliary, who never incorporates, lights cigars, cigarettes, and pipes for the Orixás, and lights candles. He or she gives them the ritual chalk called a *pemba*, with which the entity draws symbols on the ground to identify itself. The Cambone also writes down recipes and other directions that the Orixás give patients during consultations. He or she also translates the special language of the Pretos Velhos for the clients. This necessary assistance relieves the leader of these tasks and enables the leader to focus completely on the ritual at hand. The Cambone is in charge of handing over the offerings to the Orixás. In Bantu-influenced ter-reiros, the Cambone-de-Ebó renders the offering to Exu.

Ekéde

The *Ekéde*[8] organizes the public festivals and attends the mediums when they are in trance, making sure they do not fall down or bump into furniture, wiping the sweat from their faces, leading them to the dressing room, and attiring them in the style of their head entities. This woman must have the same head Orixá as the Iaôs she assists; that is, she is the filha (daughter) of the same Orixá even though she herself does not incorporate. The Ekédes care for the Orixás' clothing and props as well as the personal articles of the spiritual leader. Although they do not pass through a "head-making" initiation (see the next sec-tion) like the Iaôs, they participate in a presentation and confirmation ceremony similar to the honorary *Ogãs* (who will be descibed later in this chapter).

Dagã

This is a key post, because the *Dagã*[9] is in charge of rendering the *padê*, a special offering to Exu, and cares for the house of Exu. She is always present at the final ceremony of a session when Exu is dis-patched so he may carry out the works of the sect. The Dagã makes sure Exu's house is always clean and well lighted, and she prepares the sustenance he likes, such as *oti* (sugar cane liquor), *po pupa* (dendê oil), and *ogn* (honey). She has her own assistant, called the *Sidagā*.

Other Officers

Minor posts include that of the *Iá Tebexê*,[10] the female who leads the singing of the sacred songs. The *Iabassê*[11] is the chief cook of all the food for the Orixás, as well as the comestibles consumed during rituals or banquets for initiates, and festival food for the public. The Iabassê's duties are discussed at length in Chapter 5.

A female initiate with at least seven years experience, an *Ebâme*[12] guides the most recent members. In some Umbanda traditions, she may pass through a special ceremony after which she is able to "hive off" and create her own temple. An initiate with at least thirty years experience who helps maintain the terreiro and aids the less experienced members in their activities is called a *Vodunsi*.[13] This is not to be confused with a *Vodunsi-hunja*, a new initiate who has as yet only received the spirit of a deceased child while in trance. An *Abiã*[14] is a first-level aspirant, not yet an Iaô, but whose head Orixá has already been chosen by the shell game divination technique.

THE IAÔ AND THE HEAD-MAKING CEREMONY

The *Iaô*[15] (who is usually female, but not always) earns her status as a medium by undergoing the arduous "head-making" initiation rite, in which her Orixá takes possession of her head and after which she is bound to the deity forever. The nearest equivalent to a "head Orixá" in the Western Magickal tradition is the concept of a holy guardian angel. Even this comparison is not perfect because in the deeper realms of

Western Occultism, one's guardian angel is actually the higher self, not a separate entity.

The period of preparation for the head-making rite can take anywhere from three weeks (in some Umbanda sects) to a year (in the orthodox Gegê tradition). The aspirant sometimes is bound and sequestered in a small cell known as a *camarinha*, where her body is shaved and cut in several places. Then she bathes in herbs and in the blood of the Orixá's sacrificed animals, and the *pontos*, or invocation sigils of her head Orixá, is painted on her with a pemba (see Chapter 5 for more on pontos). Finally, the new initiate is presented before other initiates and family members in a celebratory ceremony that includes a banquet and ritual dancing.

Mediums claim that the pain they suffer is an important step toward bonding with their Orixás. The following translated excerpts from a book on Candomblé describe some of the chilling experiences from the more orthodox traditions that mediums must endure.

> In the beginning, the Iaô passes through a complete shaving, beginning with the head. The one who does the shaving is the spiritual leader, aided by the Iá Kekeré. Using special soap and a brand-new knife, they begin to shave, all the while intoning chants to the Orixás. Cuts are made with a knife on the Iaô's body to rid it of evil influences.... Rattles are tied on her legs so that she cannot flee the camarinha. If she tries, the sound will betray her and she will be punished immediately.

> Sacrificing animals on the head of the Iaô is the culminating point of the initiation. The animals are killed by the Axogun in the presence of those who are directing the ritual, and the guests and relatives of the initiate. Before the sacrifice, another officer offers the animals some herbs to eat.

The sacrificial blood runs down the Iaô's face and drenches her clothing. Then the carcasses are placed in clay vessels and are quartered and prepared for the feast which everyone consumes.[16]

THE OGÃS AND OTHER MALE OFFICIALS

Besides the Babalorixá, Babá-Kekerê, and Cambone, the Ogã[17] is probably the most important male associated with a Candomblé terreiro. I say "associated" because his title is honorary. This is a man who, because he holds a prestigious social and financial position outside the terreiro, is capable and willing to support the sect. He cannot request the position, rather the spiritual leader chooses him to receive the honor.

At his presentation, he is introduced to all the members, who stand in a circle and clap, then bow to him and ask his benediction as he passes. Six months later he is confirmed in a ceremony where he provides both feathered and hided animals for sacrifice, and is taken into the *peji* (private altar) by the leader, who offers up special prayers to the Orixás. Everyone celebrates with a banquet and ritual dances. From that time forth, the Ogã has the right to go anywhere in the temple without special authorization. When he enters the *barracão* (public salon) during a ritual, he is greeted with a special rhythm that is played for him by the drummers.

Other types of Ogãs besides the honorary patron include those who supervise and coordinate drumbeats and songs. The *Ogã-de-Terreiro* helps the chief during public ceremonies. The *Ogã Alakê* or *Ogã Calofé* is the chief drummer. This man verifies that all the songs are sung in the correct sequence. He holds a very important position because he gives general instructions to the public and directs the other drummers. He needs to know all the rhythms and all the words to all the songs of all the Orixás of the terreiro as well as those of visiting members from other groups.

The *Axogun* performs a completely different function in that he feeds and bathes the *ossé* (animal sacrifices) and possesses the *mão de faca*, the "knife hand" or permission from the Orixás that enables him to perform sacrifices. After killing the animal, he opens it and separates the entrails. He sometimes treats the hides and gives the skins to the Ogãs, who make drums from them.

Finally, the *Peji-Gã* organizes the altar and takes care that house rules are followed by all. An *Exi-de-Orixá* is the name for a general filho-de-santo, a first-level male initiate who has never passed through a head-shaving ceremony.

PRACTITIONERS

The graceful, costumed figures yield to the irresistible drumbeat in the temple. During the day in the street a majestic-looking woman, elegantly turned out from turban to toe with freshly starched white lace blouse and billowing skirt, sells Bahian "soul food" cuisine on a street corner. It is hard to imagine that these devotees are ordinary people with jobs, homes, and families, who lead everyday lives outside the terreiro. Therefore, it is important to take a look at who the practitioners are, not for sociological study, but simply to deepen our understanding and appreciation of the members of these sects.

In general, Brazil presents pretty much a hierarchical society with distinct upper, middle, and lower classes based more on economics than anything else. Even though a rigid hierarchical structure is preserved in the terreiro, it is not determined by social class, race, or sex.

All classes come together more or less as equals to participate in these spiritual rites. While Candomblé and the Amerindian religions tend to include more lower-class adherents, and Umbanda and Spiritism draw more middle-class members, in these sessions, domestic servants, school teachers, odd-jobbers, military officers, business people, skilled laborers, and high-level government officials all rub elbows.[18]

Racially, while Candomblé is more African, Caucasians and Indians are not excluded, and they have even added their own influences to all but the most traditional sects. The percentage of Whites to Blacks in Umbanda seems to reflect the population at large, although Whites (especially White males) proportionately tend to hold higher positions than their overall numbers indicate.

Diana De Groat Brown has made a study[19] of the people involved in these religions, and based on her statistics, suggests that Umbanda is not necessarily a religion that "whitens" Blacks, as has popularly been supposed.[20] She points to the large number of participating Blacks and Mulattos from the middle sectors and concludes:

> What these theories failed to take into account was that just as individuals may, at least in theory, become upwardly mobile, so may cultural practices. Umbanda, as it has gained a measure of respectability and has ceased to be identified with an exclusively Afro-Brazilian and a lower sector membership, has continued to attract upwardly mobile Blacks and mulattos.[21]

She says that she is not sure, however, if Blacks participate because it is a middle-class religion or because it celebrates their African roots. I would like to add that in Brazil, searching for one's roots—no matter the ethnic background—is not such a fervently engaged pastime as it is in the U.S.

More females participate than men, particularly in Candomblé. A prejudice exists in the general population that men who take part in

Candomblé rites are homosexuals.[22] Compared to the far greater numbers of women involved in Roman Catholicism, the relative percentages of males and females in the Afro-Brazilian religions seems more balanced. However, more men than women head terreiros, and at an earlier age than women, with the percentage of female spiritual leaders increasing with age—this, even though more older than younger males generally partake.

Participation in these religions appears to be primarily an adult activity, with the largest proportion of devotees in their thirties and forties. Mediumship under the age of eighteen, though not unheard of, is soundly discouraged. This does not imply that entire families do not join in worship. As often as not, families may be divided in their affiliations. In one family I knew, the father and three sons attended a Spiritist center every Saturday while the wife, daughter, and maid frequented a Macumba terreiro on Friday nights. The aunt, the only other family member I met, was a staunch Catholic who disapproved of her relatives' activities.

Attendees may be married, single, separated, or divorced. Although they often may have originally been brought to the terreiro by a friend, evidently they do not join in order to make and foster social relationships. They do not visit each other's houses or socialize outside their centros.

People seem drawn to these faiths for many reasons. Some come to seek help in overcoming a spiritual, physical, or financial difficulty. About ten percent of the practitioners seem motivated by a desire to help others, and an equal number cite sheer curiosity. Others say that they were originally attracted to these religions because they sought out their African or Brazilian historical roots and did not feel spiritually fulfilled by their birth religion. This attitude is similar to the opinion expressed by some practitioners of Western Witchcraft who say they feel that they have "come home" to the Craft.

An overwhelming number of people claim Catholicism as their former religion, which makes sense in a predominantly Catholic country. Still many parishioners were once Protestants or Jews. There does not seem to be any stigma attached to practicing more than one religion, since according to Brown, around half of the former Catholics still consider themselves Catholic, and most of the Jews also adhere to Judaism. About one-fifth of the mediums appear to float among various terreiros or change their terreiro affiliation from time to time. A Macumba practitioner friend of mine remarked when I saw her exiting a Catholic Church one night, "It doesn't hurt to cover all your bases." This seems to be a fairly common attitude. Then again, Brazilians have always been known for their religious tolerance. (Quite a worthy national trait, considering all the bloody wars that have been and continue to be fought in the cause of the one "true" faith.)

All in all, those who practice these religions are culled from all segments of society and make up a complex and varied tapestry of people as rich and unique as the people of Brazil. This is, as Brazilians would say, "logical," because that is who they are.

SACRED GROUND

The conversation and jostling noises in the dressing rooms have ceased. The Babalorixá, clad in clean, white cotton pants, shirt, and tennis shoes, kneels in the middle of the floor and lights a single white candle in a holder, which has been placed next to a glass of water. Like albino moths drawn to a flame, the thirty members of the sect, also dressed in white, flutter forward from the corners of the temple, and stand in a circle in rapt attention, focusing on the light. Their leader reminds them that for this very important session they must purge their thoughts of all emotions and unite as one family to become pure, disinterested vessels of spiritual energy. He intones an "Our Father," and then the following prayer for Brazil:

> *O great and good Zambi, Eternal Governor of the Infinite Space, give your people peace, work and prosperity.*
>
> *Bless our immense and beloved Brazil; give to all its sons and daughters and esteemed guests the sentiment of honor and the virtue of gratefulness.*
>
> *Help us defend our Maker's glory, and our sacred right to liberty.*
>
> *Give us abundant harvests and manufactured products so this generous country can continue to fulfill its mission of working toward human solidarity.*
>
> *Bring food to every hearth, consolation to widows and orphans, peace and tranquility to the elderly and disabled, so that every Brazilian may become an apostle of kindness, and grow toward spiritual evolution.*[23]

The overhead lights snap on and the priest goes to the main door of the temple. From his pocket, he takes a white pemba—a chalky substance made from pulverized cinnamon, nutgrass, frankincense powder, ginger, river clay, star anise, and wax—and traces a mysterious sigil on the ground to keep away negativity and imbalance from the sacred space.

He returns to the altar and censes it and all the participants, then offers up a special prayer to Archangel Michael to protect the incarnate and discarnate souls and each "child of the saint" who will participate in tonight's ritual. He finishes with this prayer:

Hail to Faith, Hope, and Charity!
Hail to the Legions of Umbanda and Quimbanda!
Blessings be to Zambi and Ifá, the Divine Holy Ghost!

Off to the side, the drums start beating, softly at first, then louder and more insistently. The prayers offered by the Babalorixá come faster and more urgently now. Beads of sweat begin to form on his forehead, and the Ekéde rushes to press them away with a white towel.

Prayers are offered in song to Ogum, the chief spirit guide of the terreiro, to Oxalá, Iemanjá, Oxóssi, and all the Orixás and entities who will soon descend to the sacred space. The Iaôs dance furiously to the urgent beat, and the door is opened for the public to timidly file in and wait the coming of the saints.

Thus begins a charity session in an Umbanda temple. The entities who will incorporate tonight freely give consultations and advice to the public in an effort to improve their lives.

Rituals take place in the sacred space of the terreiro, which may also go by many names, including *centro* (center), *templo* (temple), *tenda* (tent), *cabana*, or *roça* (clearing in the woods). Whatever name the congregation uses, it refers both to the area where the entities take possession of their mediums and to the establishment itself.

As you learned in Chapter 1, the oldest terreiro in Brazil, from which all the others are alleged to have originated, is the Candomblé Casa Branca de Engenho Velho (White House of the Old Mill), founded in 1830 in Salvador. The oldest temple in Rio de Janeiro was initially founded as a Kardecist Center in 1908. Usually the establishments are named for the patron entity, for example, Centro de Ogum Marê (Center of Ogum of the Tide).

The look of the temple varies considerably depending on the tradition, relative wealth of the members, and whether it is located in an urban, small town, or rural setting. I have visited terreiros large enough to accommodate one hundred dancers and attended sessions held in private homes with only a few participants.

As mentioned before, Spiritist centers are decorated plainly and simply, adorned only with a table covered by a white cloth, and chairs where the mediums and visitors sit. If the tradition is very African, there are two altars. One is located in the *barracão*[24] or public salon. Another, called a peji,[25] is hidden deep within the recesses of the building where the public and perhaps many of the parishioners are not allowed. This altar contains protective symbols, otás (holy stones),[26] and fetishes that contain the axé of the terreiro. Sacred food for the Orixás is also placed on the altar. Thus the peji serves as the seat of the group's power.

Terreiro layouts vary considerably depending on the number of members and their means. I will describe to you the terreiro in Rio that I visited most often, as it is as typical an example as any other. Figure 1 shows the layout.

Terreiro Ogum Beira-Mar (Seaside Ogum) is divided into consultation room, dressing rooms, kitchen, several side altars for the Orixás and souls of recently "passed over" (deceased) members and their families, and a special altar-cubicle for Exu at the entrance.

In the main part of the temple, which can be closed or opened for public view, are the main altar, area for musicians, and directory. At the directory, the public can pick up consultation numbers and leave gifts for the Orixás. The month's program is posted there, as well as the names of the mediums and other initiates, and the entities with which the mediums work.

There is also a large section of benches set aside for the congregation (often separating men and women, but not in this center) that is divided by banisters from the central area. This portion of the room has a dirt floor about twenty meters square where dancing and spirit possessions occur. Together these sections form the barracão. The roof

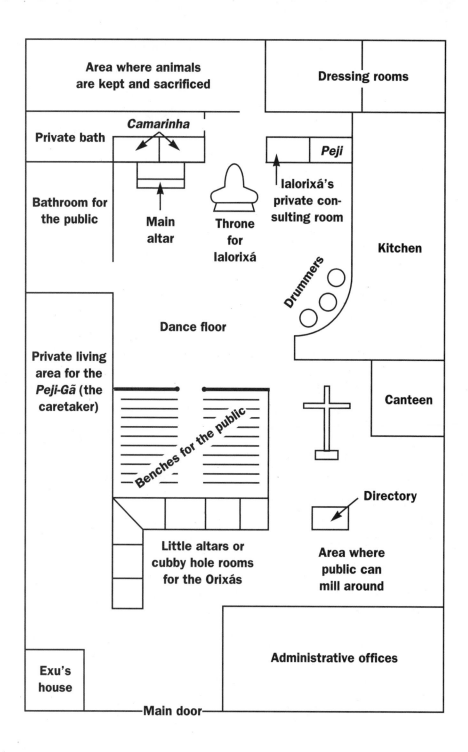

Figure 1: Layout of a typical terreiro.

of this central section thrusts upward and is made from straw and hung with colorful raffia and fringe. The walls are decorated with pictures of the Orixás and other entities. This establishment also has an enormous cross about five meters high that stands by the entrance to the central area.

At the front of the building is the administrative director's office, who, in this case, is not the spiritual leader because she works a full-time day job. Off to the side sits a little canteen where the public can buy light refreshments and non-alcoholic beverages for themselves, and alcoholic beverages and offerings such as cigars, cigarettes, rum, and perfumes for the entities. These items are sold at low prices because the purpose of the shop, rather than to make money, is to provide a place where the public can buy necessary items without having to leave the terreiro and venture out into a rough neighborhood. (This center, like so many others, is located in the North Zone of Rio, infamous for its high crime rate.)

The private sanctuary at the back, entered through double doors, houses the peji, which, as previously described, holds the statues, stones, and symbols of the Orixás. In the back of the building, animals—mostly birds—are kept for sacrifice. Nearby is the *roncó*,[28] the little chamber where acolytes are sequestered while undergoing initiation procedures. This is where the initiate is cleansed and purified and taught the secrets and rituals of the sect.

Occasionally, the spiritual leaders may live in the building, especially if it is the person's home, but more often the terreiro remains deserted except during sessions. Such is the case with Ogum Beira-Mar. Establishments are often located in rural or remote urban neighborhoods in order to minimize complaints from neighbors about the loud drumming and singing. Those who see a pronounced political reflection in these organizations claim that the power elite forces the terreiros into remote areas in order to minimize their importance.

The stage has been set, and you are familiar with the players. In the next chapter, you will learn about some of the more dramatic practices of these sects.

NOTES

1. *Ialorixá* comes from the Yoruba words *iya*, "mother," and *orissá*, "divinity." In Portuguese, the term *mãe-de-santo* is also used and signifies "mother of the saint."

2. *Babalorixá* is a Yoruba combination of *babá*, "father," and *alá*, "possessor, awe" or "possessor of an awesome power." In Portuguese, the expression is *pai-de-santo* or "father of the saint." Sometimes he is also called a *Babalâo*. Traditionally, only the Babalâo could throw the cowrie shells because he was a priest of Ifá, the Orixá of divination, but these days Babalorixás can also divine with the shells.

3. *Assentamento*, also *assento* from the Portuguese, means "fixing" or "the act of passing action into an object." Any representation of an Orixá can be fixed through ritual with the power of the entity. Examples include *otás* (power stones; see note 26), ritual instruments rendered in miniature, botanicals, et cetera. These symbols are steeped in dendê oil, honey, or other liquids to trap the power.

4. *Babá-Kekerê*, from the Yoruba word *kekerê*, means "little." In Portuguese, the term is *pai pequeno*, "little father." *Iá-Kekerê* in Portuguese is *mãe pequena*, "little mother."

5. Personal hygiene is very important to Brazilians. Because they live in a tropical climate and because bathing water is often difficult for the poor to come by, whether or not a person takes the time and effort to care for personal cleanliness shows a lot about the individual's character. Personal hygiene is so important that in the Afro-Brazilian religions it is equated with good moral fiber.

6. *Ialaxé*, from the Yoruba *ia*, "mother," *la*, "great," and *axé*, "power" means "mother of the great power."

7. *Cambono* is a Kimbundu language word for "little Black person." *Cambono* is a male, *Cambona* is a female, and sometimes *Cambone* is used for both genders.

8. *Ekéde*, sometimes spelled *Ekédi*, combines the Yoruba words *eké*, "support," and *di*, "to become," meaning "to become an aid or support to someone." These assistants are also known as *Yabás* or *Ilaís* in Xangô rituals of the Northeast.

9. *Dagã* originates in the Yoruba words *dá*, "to become," and *ogá*, "a superior person" or "chief."

10. *Iá Tebexê* is Yoruba for "mother who makes the propitiary supplications."

11. *Iabassê* in the Yoruba language means "matron of the kitchen."

12. *Ebâme*, also spelled *Ebâmi* or *Ebômim* in Yoruba, means "someone on whom a mark has been definitively made."

13. *Vodunsi* is roughly translated from a term in the Ewe language meaning "wife of the Orixás."

14. *Abiã* is from a Yoruba term *abé*, meaning "beneath," because she is on the lowest rung of the hierarchy.

15. *Iaô*, also spelled *Yaô*, *Yawô* in Yoruba means "bride."

16. Fernandes Portugal, *Encantos e Magia dos Orixás no Candomblé* (Rio de Janeiro: Editora Tecnoprint, S.A., 1986), 67–68.

17. *Ogã* in Yoruba means "superior person" or "chief."

18. An exception occurs in those terreiros in which an influential man becomes an *Ogã* or benefactor. This concept is an extension of the old Colonial patronage system.

19. Diana De Groat Brown, *Umbanda: Religion and Politics in Urban Brazil* (Ann Arbor, MI: UMI Research Press, 1986).

20. Umbanda has been accused by proponents of Macumba and Quimbanda of bending to the conservative dictates of repressive governments, especially when Brazil was under military rule, by discouraging any religious behavior that would be distasteful or seem the product of an underdeveloped, unprogressive nation. According to this bias, Blacks who embrace Umbanda would be making a statement that they were giving up their cultural roots in order to be accepted by the White establishment.

21. Brown, *Umbanda: Religion and Politics in Urban Brazil*, 131.

22. This idea may be based on the fact that in Candomblé when male mediums incorporate female entities, they often exhibit exaggeratedly feminine traits. Although Brazil is not an extremely macho culture, it is mildly so, especially among the lower classes from which many of Candomblé's adherents are drawn. Also, some predominantly male homosexual Candomblé terreiros do exist, and people know about them.

23. Pompílio Possera de Eufrázio, *Catecismo do Umbandista* (Rio de Janeiro: Editora Eco, 1974), 18–19.

24. The word *barracão* means "large shack" in Portuguese.

25. The term *peji* has a possible origin in the Yoruba words *pé*, "to call, invite," and *ji*, "to give a present" or *pèje*, "an invitation to attend a banquet."

26. An otá is a stone that is ritually instilled with an Orixá's vital force. Each Orixá is associated with a different stone. Examples include lead, lodestone, marble, seashells, or rocks collected from riverbeds or the forest.

27. The word *roncó* in Yoruba combines *ró*, "to show the path," with *n* (a present participle), and *có*, "to teach," all meaning "showing or teaching the path of spiritual development." This room is also called by a Portuguese word *camarinha*, meaning "little chamber."

CHAPTER 5

UNIQUE PRACTICES

Have you ever dared invoke the horned, red-skinned, cloven-hoofed god? Some Brazilians petition Exu to help them in their lives. Here's how they do it.

TO OPEN YOUR PATHS

To begin this spell,[1] gather together the following ingredients to make an offering to Exu of the Seven Crossroads: seven matchboxes; seven cigars; seven black-and-red candles; a long red, black, and white piece of cloth; a handful of yellow corn, a bottle of cachaça,[2] one portion of *farofa de dendê* (see Appendix D); and one portion of *canjica* (corn cooked with salt) contained in a casserole dish. Also fill a bottle with water and cap it.

Wrap everything in a bundle, and go to a crossroads. Take out the bottle of water, kneel down, and spill some on the ground three times, first in front of you, then to your left, then to your right.

In your mind's eye, picture Exu of the Seven Crossroads with his pointed ears and beard. He is enveloped in an enormous red cape, with seven crosses springing from the ground at his feet. Invoke this lusty entity with these words:

> ***The one who decants water before him/herself***
> ***Will walk on fertile ground.***

Make a fist with the hand you use least. Dip the fingers of the hand you use most in one of the wet spots you made on the ground. After you moisten your fingers, strike the palm of your open hand against your closed fist. Repeat the procedure with the other two wet spots. The last time you strike your fist, open your hand and say:

> ***Three times I invoke you, Exu of the Seven Crossroads,***
> ***Three times as if they were one!***

Lay out the cloth on the ground in front of you and arrange on top of it the items you have brought for the offering. Light the candles, open the matchboxes near the cigars, and let the match heads protrude. Open the bottle of cachaça, set it down, and place the dish of corn in front of it. Sprinkle the farofa de dendê on top of the canjica. Stand with the dish of canjica in both your hands, and extend your arms straight out in front of you over the rest of the offering. In this way you honor your future.

Next, you need to honor your past. Transfer the dish of canjica to one hand, move it carefully behind your back with bent elbow, then grab onto the casserole dish with both hands. Once you have the bowl of canjica safely secured in both hands, extend your arms behind you as straight as you can. Repeat the same gesture with outstretched arms holding the canjica to your right, thereby celebrating the astral world, and finally to your left, in homage to the material world.

Deposit the dish of canjica in the center of the cloth, by way of saluting the present. Say:

> *May the earth bear witness that in this place I* [say your name] *salute the powers of all the Exus. With these gestures I forge a link in the present time with my ancestors from the past so that Exu of the Seven Crossroads, who knows everything about my past, may chart my future and my path. Exu, I entreat you to knock down the barriers, fill the potholes, drive away my enemies, and any and all instability, envy, sickness, and fear that blocks the road!*

OFFERINGS

No matter what the tradition, offerings to the divine potencies compose an indispensable part of Afro-Brazilian ritual. The previous story shows how offerings are used in spellwork to request something of the gods, in this case, to free the petitioner from the restrictions imposed either by oneself or by black magick perpetrated by others, and to open one's path in order to achieve life's fullest potential.

Sometimes offerings are simply made in homage to the Orixás, for example, at their annual feast days. Every divinity is especially honored once a year in very much the same way we celebrate birthdays. During the ceremony, food and other offerings are laid on the altar by the feet of the divinity. These happy occasions, such as the Iemanjá Day mentioned in Chapter 2, are often enjoyed by the public. Another public ceremony occurs when a new medium is initiated. Friends and relatives are invited to the terreiro, and a great banquet is held. Part of this banquet is presented to the reigning Orixá of the medium's head.

At other times, the offerings are rendered privately by the medium for his or her head Orixá. The medium presents the food and other offertory objects on the appropriate platters to the entity at the main altar in its "house," which is a cubicle-like altar room within the terreiro. It is usually flanked by shutters so it can be opened or closed from public view. Filhos-de-santo have what is known as an "obligation" to make offerings as often as weekly to their Orixás in order to strengthen the bonds between initiates and their gods. However, you don't have to be an initiate to make a petition and offering. Here is an example of how you go about it.

How to Land a Good Job

Prepare an *axoxô* for Oxóssi. One of his favorite foods, an axoxô consists of yellow corn mixed with coconut. On another dish, mix together shelled, crushed peanuts and honey. Take these dishes to your altar along with a bottle of cachaça, a little clay pot filled with honey, and seven silver coins. Offer them all to Oxóssi, and compose a personal prayer to him to grant your request.

▲ ▲ ▲

Thanksgiving offerings are also tendered when an entity complies with a petitioner's request. In fact, in some traditions, it is believed that offerings should not be made in advance to a Pomba-Gira or else she may not fulfill the wish. It is also said that Pomba-Gira actually prefers to be recompensed for a task successfully completed because the reward from the grateful petitioner will be that much greater.

More often than not, an offering requires that food and drink be prepared. In the Afro-Brazilian system, it is believed that if in the mundane world the purpose of good food, dancing, and fraternization is to bring about happiness and well-being, then the same methods will hold true in the spiritual realm. A lively "party" will attract the entities, who will enjoy themselves and be happily disposed to confer positive energy on the members of the gathering.

As with all aspects of Afro-Brazilian ritual, exacting procedures are strictly followed when the food is prepared. The Iabassê, or chief cook, whom you met in Chapter 4, is in charge of all the cooking and supervision of assistants. She and her helpers must be "clean"—they cannot be menstruating, and they cannot have indulged in alcohol or had sexual intercourse within the previous twenty-four hours. They dress in ritual robes and wear their *guias*, the beaded necklaces that link them to their head Orixás.

All food, whether destined for the gods or their worshippers, is prepared in clay pots over wood or coal fires. (No cheating with electric, gas, or kerosene!) Pots are stirred with a wooden spoon in a circular motion beginning on the right side and moving counterclockwise around to the left. Back-and-forth or straight left-to-right motions across the pot are not to be tolerated. During food preparation, as in so many other aspects of the ritual, sacred songs are sung to the Orixás.

The Iabassê is conversant with the favorite foods of all the Orixás and entities cultivated in her terreiro, and prepares everything for private and public ceremonies as well as for the annual feasts. She may also cook the *quitutes*, Afro-Bahian delicacies that are sold at stands in the street to raise money for the terreiro or for charity. (Speaking as one who has lived in both Mexico—where I would never eat street food—and Brazil, I recommend that if you find yourself traveling to Brazil, you try this food. It is prepared under hygienic conditions with a great deal of care. Although there may be exceptions, I, for one, have never gotten sick eating quitutes.)

Once the meal is ready, the spiritual leader may throw the cowrie shells to see whether the food has been accepted by the divinity. If not, it is divided among the worshippers, and another batch is prepared—this time even more laboriously.

Let me describe to you a banquet for Oxum that I once attended. I came only for the ritual meal, so did not have a chance to watch the Iabassê and Iabôs prepare the *omolucum* (a dish of French beans and eggs with salt, shrimp, and dendê) and other dishes, but I did see the food leave the kitchen.

When I arrived, the drums were already throbbing and members of the sect were singing songs of praise for this pretty goddess of fresh water, stream, and rivers. A mechanical waterfall had been erected against a wall of the barracão, but I could not hear its tinkling over the music and incantations.

The cook's helpers left the kitchen and thoroughly swept the floor of the main room. Then they unfurled a large straw mat over which they laid a long blue tablecloth painted with the invocation signs, symbols, and sigils of Oxum. They set a glass of fresh spring water directly in the center of the cloth and flanked it with two pitchers filled with the same liquid. This was for the diners to partake of, because it is Oxum's favorite drink. The attendants then brought steaming platters of corn cooked with coconut, omolucum, French beans, yams cooked with rice, as well as hard-boiled eggs, fresh bananas, papayas, and *lelê* (caramelized, sweetened evaporated milk with coconut pieces) from the kitchen and laid them on the table.

At that moment, the Ogã Calofé motioned for the drums to cease, and everybody took their places. Everyone partook of the omolucum, but different parts of the cooked and seasoned hen were reserved for members in accordance with their status in the terreiro's hierarchy. Before beginning to eat, the spiritual leader invoked Oxum with her salutation, *Eri ieiê ô!* First the leader took a bite of food, then her assistants took a bite. Then the entire group set to eating in complete silence with only the murmuring of the waterfall as a background.

When the meal was over, the Iá Kekerê said something in Yoruba that I did not understand, but which became evident as a signal for everyone to rise. This ended official celebratory meal and ritual.

Afro-Brazilian cuisine, sometimes known as Afro-Bahian cooking because the dishes mainly originate in that state, is the best ethnic food in Brazil. It has been praised in international cookbooks and even in literature. Thirty years before the publication of *Like Water for Chocolate* by Mexican writer Laura Esquivel, Jorge Amado, a novelist from Bahia, wrote delightful books such as *Gabriela Clove and Cinnamon* and *Dona Flor and Her Two Husbands* (mentioned in Chapter 1), which metaphorically incorporate Bahian recipes into the themes and plots.

The dishes of the many entities differ somewhat from tradition to tradition and even from centro to centro. Sometimes the divinities accept fruit and beverages. Drinks, called *curiadore*s, are non-alcoholic in the more traditional temples, but under the influence of the Caboclo and Indian sects of the North, more and more terreiros now offer alcoholic curiadores, such as champagne, wine, brandy, and cachaça to their gods. Appendix D describes the ingredients of some of the more common dishes and names the entities with whom they are linked.

SACRIFICE

The topic of offertory food naturally leads to a discussion of the controversial practice of animal sacrifice, which is portrayed in the following vignette.

The day dawned gray and cold after the night's torrential rainstorm. Dressed in a simple white shirt and pants, the Axogun with the long, curly, black hair—chief sacrificer of the terreiro—padded barefoot through the morning mist to the enclosure where the livestock were kept. He carried in his hand a long, sharp knife. He did not smile as he took the black cock from its cage.

This man with the serious eyes and steady hand began singing a low and steady chant as he patiently and thoroughly washed the cock's beak and claws. Tenderly, he secured the claws with a red ribbon. As the first rays of the new day struck through the fog and penetrated into the recesses of the room, he raised the knife and swiftly severed the bird's head at the neck.

"The head," he thought to himself, "for thought and vision."

He untied the claws of the lifeless animal and cut them off "for walking," he muttered, and the wings "for flight." Then he opened the bird and separated the heart, lungs, and brains "for vitality." (If it had been a four-footed animal, he would have removed the tail "for direction and equilibrium.")

The Axogun carefully arranged the body parts on a platter and silently delivered the dish to the Babalorixá, who threw the cowrie shells to see if the sacrifice was accepted. After a tense moment, the answer came: "Yes, Exu has found the sacrifice to his liking."

Later that night at the temple's weekly charity session, the "Dispatching of Exu" rite started off the ceremony. The Babalorixá pulled a curtain across the main altar that housed all the Orixás. He lit a candle and set it in the middle of the main salon floor next to a clay pitcher brimming with pure spring water. The drum tempo changed, and the worshippers all turned toward the main door. They began to sing praises of Exu and the "People of the Street," begging the entity not to disturb the proceedings and to expeditiously carry the believers' petitions to the gods. Then the Dagã, caretaker of Exu's altar, took the water outside and poured it on the ground to propitiate the congregation's ancestors.

▲ ▲ ▲

The scene presented above describes Exu's padê, a sacrificial offering to this entity, which is practiced by many Afro-Brazilian sects at the beginning of public and private services. First, the sacrifice of a black cock is made at dawn, and the offering is presented at Exu's altar along with farofa fried in dendê oil. The rest of the offering, accompanied by songs of praise and petitions, initiates the public ceremony later the same night.

To those involved in Western Magickal Mystery Traditions such as Wicca, or in standard Judeo-Christian sects, the idea of sacrificing animals to appease the gods seems abhorrent. From an early age, most Westerners are taught that we are the guardians of wildlife and domestic animals, that it is our responsibility to respect, protect, and care for them; and that we should never, ever harm them. I must admit that as a child of my culture, I have not been able to overcome my "gut" revulsion to animal sacrifice as practiced in the Afro-Brazilian religions, and I have never yet been able to bring myself to witness the event. However, I do not think that the people who practice this rite (within the Brazilian context only) are evil, and I have struggled hard to mentally understand their point of view. Let me see if I can explain their stance as I see it.

In the first place, any member of an Afro-Brazilian sect would tell you that all religions, including the Judaism and Christianity of the Bible, and Wicca in times gone by, have relied on ritual sacrifices and offerings to propitiate their gods. Not only have they sacrificed animals (Christians and Jews seemed to particularly favor lambs), but sometimes human beings as well. (For example, the Wicker Man of Celtic Britain was sacrificed so that the harvest would be bountiful, or Odin of Norse legend sacrificed himself to gain the secrets of the runes for humanity.) The Catholic-Protestant custom of tithing to the Church presents a modern-day example of yet another kind of sacrifice.

Worshippers of the Orixás are quick to point out Westerners' hypocrisy. In their opinion, the wafer and wine offered up at communion is the same as any botanical sacrifice. The Christian custom of eating lamb at Easter and turkey, ham, or roast beef at Christmas involves killing animals. Christians just don't usually kill the animals themselves unless they live on a farm, but prefer to get their sacrifices plastic-wrapped from the grocery store. Followers of Afro-Brazilian teachings will tell you that at least they personally care for the animals. These animals are not being corralled into stinking, terrifying, inhumane slaughterhouses as happens elsewhere in the Western world. Their sacrifices usually include fowl and an occasional goat or sheep, and the killing is done with great respect for the animal by a very competent sacrificer who must serve a long apprenticeship. One of this person's chief tasks is to inflict as little pain as possible on the victim.

Adherents of Afro-Brazilian sects will underscore that they do not and never have sacrificed humans, nor have they ever expected obligatory tithes from anyone. (Although mediums and other believers must perform "obligations," which, by the time they acquire the necessary offertory ingredients, can run into quite a bit of money.) Adherents believe that just as burning incense or offertory herbs releases the life force, or axé, of plants, so the letting of the animal's blood releases its axé. The axé that was instilled in this life form by the Orixás returns to the divinities to "feed" their energies so they continue to be potent. Stated another way, the members of these sects believe that the act of sacrifice to the Orixás helps keep the earth's cycles moving and maintains a balance between humans and nature that, in the end, celebrates life.

Mário César Barcellos eloquently sums up the Afro-Brazilian stance as follows:

> In one way or another, the Earth will (always) feed on living beings (animals, vegetables, humans). However, the Afro-Brazilian transforms this into a sacred ritual where he shows an enormous respect for the Earth and its powers, for the life that he is extinguishing, for the act of being alive and able to feed himself and his kin....[3]

Those of you intrigued by Afro-Brazilian religions and philosophy, but who still cannot accept animal sacrifice, take heart! Reasonable botanical substitutes for animal sacrifices have been created by U.S. Americans who practice these religions.[4] In any case, as you will find out presently, offerings of all sorts are made on various occasions, particularly those that involve personal spellwork, and most of these offerings do not require harming a hair of any wee little beastie's head.

SPELLWORK

Spells,[5] which often include an offering to an Orixá or other spiritual entity, are widely performed both by practitioners and the public at large. Recall from the beginning of the book the well-dressed young woman who made an offering on the median strip of a busy highway. She is typical of the sort of person who may perform spellwork. The public who attend open rituals like the charity session you read about in Chapter 4 go to receive advice from entities who often will recommend that the clients perform certain spells. It is said that during the years of the dictatorship in Brazil, generals and other military leaders regularly visited terreiros to receive advice about casting spells that had the purpose of keeping them in power. The ploy may have worked because the military miraculously stayed in control between 1964 and 1985. The military's "Macumba habit" seems to have spilt over to the civilian government, because in the last days of his presidency before he was impeached, Fernando Collor (president from 1991 to 1992) was accused in the press of the same sort of behavior.

These mini-rituals, such as the one cited at the beginning of this chapter, are performed for an infinite number of purposes from the highest to the basest. People work spells to procure love, money, better health, and legal aid; to protect or banish negativity from their environment; to develop spirituality or psychic abilities; and also, alas, sometimes to control, compel, or injure someone else.

However, most of the members of the Brazilian sects believe in working magick purely for benevolent purposes, and warn against performing negative spells. For example, José Ribeiro, known as the King Solomon of Brazilian Umbanda, is adamant in his condemnation of black magick when he says:

> It does no good to practice evil because of the Law of return; that is to say, the evil that we send to our enemies returns to us. If the reader has suffered an injustice, or has been the object of a Black Magick spell, present your case before Zambi. He will assure that justice is done.... Sooner or later we always pay our debts. This planet is one of trials. Here we suffer, here we learn, and we return as many times as necessary for our spirits to evolve. So it is not useful for us to seek vengeance in this incarnation. Such inferior thoughts will delay our spiritual evolution and help keep us imprisoned in the material world.[6]

Some spells are short and simple, requiring little more than a glass of water, a candle or a box of matches, and a prayer from the heart. Others include more complex ingredients such as specially prepared food and drink and sigils drawn on cloth. Some rely on certain spoken formulas thought to have acquired incomparable potency over the ages. Some are meant to be performed at home, while others require that the petitioner journey to the temple or sacred outdoor site such as a waterfall, forest, or ocean. Many spells to Exu take place at a four-way crossroads, while Pomba-Gira prefers the spot where two streets form a "T."

Spells include ingredients such as candles, botanicals, mojo bags, and invocation formulas that will be familiar to anyone who has

AN EXAMPLE OF A STREET RITUAL. The author performs street ritual to Pomba-Gira Maria Padilha—a ritual to attract a lover. The ritual takes place at the "T" of two crossroads, and requires seven lighted red candles, seven matches protruding from the matchbox, seven well-opened roses, and an offertory bottle of anisette liqueur.

worked magick in the Western Mystery Tradition. Some of the items—pembas (colored chalk pieces); Afro-Bahian dishes, including corn, honey, and yams; different colored ribbons; and cowrie shells—are unique to Brazilian magick. Here are several examples of spells that are typically performed. Descriptions of unfamiliar food ingredients can be found in Appendix D.

To Find a Lover

1 bottle of guaraná or a substitute

1 brand-new pen

1 clean piece of white paper

Buy a bottle of guaraná soda pop. If you do not live in Brazil or cannot find it at a speciality food store, substitute a fruity soft drink or any kind of sticky sweet carbonated drink, such as cream soda. Drink half the bottle. Taking the pen, write a short description of the kind of person you would like to meet, or if the person is known, his or her name. Below the description, write your name and the future lover's name, or a description of the unknown lover distilled into a couple of words in the form of a cross. Pray to the Ibêji:

> *I invoke you, Ibêji, with love and joy in my heart so you may come to my aid and make* [the person's name, or if unknown, "my soul mate lover"] *fall in love with me soon. Once you have worked your magick for me, I promise that I will make an offering to you of another half bottle of sweet guaraná.*

Take the half-filled bottle to any plaza or place it where pedestrians pass by frequently, and leave it with your petition secured under the bottle. Don't forget to complete the bargain you made with the Ibêji!

To Improve Your Life (I)

1   yam

1/2   pound beef giblets

Buy a yam and cut it into twenty little pieces. Add them to the giblets. Take the offering to the sea and pray to Ogum Beira-Mar (Seaside Ogum) to improve your life. If you live somewhere landlocked, such as Kansas, fill a glass with water, add some salt, and stir. Place the glass on a pile of play sand, and pretend you are at the seaside. You could also wait until you take a vacation to the ocean.

To Improve Your Life (II)

7   long-stemmed white roses,
    denuded of thorns

1   dram rose or musk perfume

1   yard white ribbon

1   yard light blue ribbon

1   white candle

1   blue candle

    matches

Rub the roses one by one over your body. While you are doing this, pray to Iemanjá to bring you good health, wealth, luck, and happiness. Next sprinkle the perfume on the petals. Using the ribbon, gather the roses and tie them together with a bow.

Take the bouquet, candles, and matches to the seashore. Affix the candles in the sand and light them. Then wade into the sea. When the seventh wave caresses your body, lay (don't throw) the bouquet in the water as an offering to Iemanjá. Let the candles burn down to the ground.

To Enlarge Your Breasts

7   grains of yellow corn

2   red candles

2   black candles

1   black dove

7   long-stemmed red roses, denuded of thorns

1   bottle of anisette liqueur

    matches

On a Friday night, take the grains of corn, one candle of each color, and the matches to a "T" crossroads. Light the candles and invoke the Pomba-Gira Maria Padilha (Mary Little Sandalfoot). Show her the corn and entreat her to imbue it with the power to make your breasts grow. Tell her that if she helps out you will give her a fine present. Leave the candles burning as an offering, and return home and rub each grain all over your breasts in large, circular motions. Continue to rub your breasts with the corn for seven Fridays in a row. On the last Friday, give the corn to the black dove to eat. By now you should see some difference in breast size.

Go back to the same "T" crossroads, taking with you the two remaining candles, matches, anisette liqueur, and seven well-opened, dethorned, long-stemmed roses. Light the candles, invoke Maria Padilha, and thank her for her assistance. Open the bottle of anisette liqueur, take a sip as a libation to the entity, and leave the bottle upright and open at the crossroads for her. Give the roses to her as a present as well. Exit the site leaving the offering and candles burning.

For Protection

pinch each of *Sansieveria ceylanica*
(St. George's Sword), rue, California pepper
tree leaves (you can substitute the leaves
from any hot pepper), Guinea hen weed,
and any type of ivy

1   bottle of holy water (water blessed by
    a Roman Catholic priest, Wiccan priest/ess
    or Afro-Brazilian spiritual leader)

1   open cowrie shell (insert the end of a metal
    file or screwdriver in the opening to crack
    the shell and "open" it)

1   yellow oleander seed

1   old penny

1   leather mojo bag

1   dram vial of mercury

Make a juice from the pinches of herbs and the holy water. Pass the
juice through a coffee filter or a piece of muslin to remove most of the
plant matter. Drop the shell, seed, and coin into the juice and let them
steep for twenty-four hours. Then take the three objects and place
them inside the mojo bag, along with the unopened dram vial of mercury. Close the sack and pray to your head Orixá or guardian angel to
protect you from all forms of negativity. Carry the bag with you in
pocket or purse, or leave it on your altar. When you no longer feel a
need for protection, dispose of the mojo bag by burying it at the foot of
a large tree.

To "Exchange Your Head"

No, this is not some sort of psychedelic spell from the days of Jefferson Airplane, but a way to counter psychic attack or terrible physical illness. Perform this spell only if you are in dire need, for to act otherwise will dilute its efficacy.

1   potted rue plant (*Ruta graveolens*)

1   white bowl filled with white corn
    or rice cooked without salt, or
    munguzaná as an offering to Oxalá

Sit in a chair with the plant on a table by your side and the offering to Oxalá on your lap, and invoke this great divine potency. Press your hands to your forehead if the malady is psychically induced, or to the place where you feel the pain if the disease is physical. Mentally will your malaise to be transferred from your head to your hands. Then place your hands on the leaves of the plant and transfer the negative energy to it by the force of your will. Now raise the offering from your lap to your forehead three times in silent thanks to Oxalá.

Take both the plant and the offering to a cemetery. Plant the rue in the sacred ground, being sure to water it well, and leave the offering to Oxalá by its side. The rue plant will absorb your negativity without harming itself because of its special ability to dissolve negativity.

In black magick, instead of rue, an offering might be prepared for Exu, which would include his food plus a handful of pins. Then the name of another person to whom the afflicted one wants to transfer the negativity might be written on a piece of paper and dropped inside the food. If the afflicted one can't think of a specific victim, the offering would be placed at a busy pedestrian crossroads, perhaps along with enough money to attract a greedy passerby. The first person to touch the money or even inadvertently step on the offering, will "exchange his/her head" with the afflicted one, and come down with the same illness and trouble. Besides reverence, this is another reason most people give street offerings wide berth.

Offering to Oxalá for Those Born under the Zodiac Sign of Leo

In the Afro-Brazilian belief system, those born under the sign of Leo are protected by Oxalá.[7] To honor the King of the Orixás, gather together the following ingredients:

1	white altar cloth
4	white china bowls
1	loaf of white bread
	sweet oil (pure, rectified olive oil, which is available at most pharmacies)
	white grape juice
	uncarbonated mineral water
4	yellow pembas (colored chalk)
6	white lilies
1	vase filled with water
6	uncolored beeswax candles in holders
	matches

On a Sunday during the waxing moon, remove all objects from your altar and cover it with the white cloth (or you can perform the ritual out-of-doors on a mat of fresh green foliage). Place three of the bowls on the cloth forming a triangle that points to the back of the altar (see Figure 2, page 118). Put the bread in one bowl, the sweet oil in another, and the grape juice in the third bowl. Set the fourth bowl in the center of the triangle, and fill it with the uncarbonated mineral water. Place the pembas around the outside of the triangle. Put the lilies in the vase at the back of the altar. Line the six candles across the front of the altar, and light them. Recite or sing the following prayer to Oxalá:

> *Oxalá, my father!*
> *Have pity on me.*
> *If the world patrol*[8] *is great*
> *Your power is even greater!*[9]

Save the original water from the vase for a purification bath and the pembas to use in future protection rituals. At the end of the ritual, remove everything but the vase of lilies from the altar.

When the lilies begin to fade, take them, the bread, juice, water, and oil, and return them to Mother Earth by burying them in the ground. Recite a personal prayer of thanksgiving to her for her bounty.

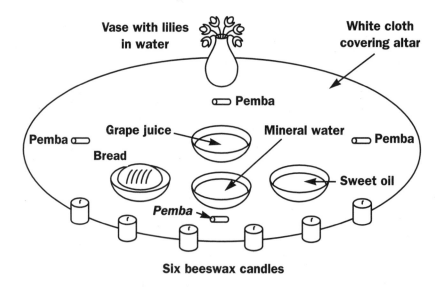

Figure 2: Arrangement of objects on the altar for an offering to Oxalá (for those born under the zodiac sign of Leo).

PEMBAS

The previous spell introduces the pemba, which is a unique feature of Afro-Brazilian ritual. A pemba is a natural mineral chalk that can be tinted different colors and magnetized to fulfill a variety of magickal purposes. Sometimes the chalk is ground together with other substances, such as herbs, seeds, stones, shells, essences, pulverized metals, animal bones, dried blood, and salt, to produce a blowing powder. The powder can be moistened and applied to cloth, metal, or other objects that have been previously engraved with the appropriate markings.

The origin of the pemba is said to be on an island near Zanzibar off the coast of Africa. Here the "true pemba" was said to be pulverized from a certain sacred stone by virgins who sang consecration songs to it while they worked. The powder was then stirred into a mucilage made from gum arabic and water, then dried and rolled into banana leaves. It was exported to Bahia at very high prices.

Given the prohibitive price of African pembas, Brazilians soon learned to make their own by using natural vegetable dyes to color powdered calcium carbonate and gum arabic or casein mucilage. They shaped the mass into cones, and dried them to form the pembas. These days, some terreiros simply use colored school chalk.

The signs and sigils that are written with pembas while a medium is possessed by a spirit are believed to be the actual script of the entity communicating from the astral world and assimilating into the chalk. The pemba, then, becomes a power source. This is why one author in the field says that the pemba is "without a doubt the most powerful instrument in Umbanda, for without the sigils (made manifest in the temple) nothing would be able to be accomplished with assurance."[10]

Through the pemba, the medium can contact the astral world by invocation, and in return, the spirits of that realm can make themselves known to the material world by manifesting through the chalk. The medium magnetizes the chalk through an act of will, which is performed during a ritual. Then he or she acts out the specific intent of calling upon the entity by drawing the invocational symbol with the pemba. This is why once the chalk has been magnetized, only the medium is allowed to touch it—no one but the magnetizer knows its true purpose. For example, a medium may magnetize a pemba with the idea of going into a trance and receiving an astral entity who will help the medium free him/herself or another person from an obsessed spirit. An entity will manifest and identify itself by drawing a sigil on the ground or a cloth with the chalk by the medium's hand. The entity proceeds to heal the patient through the medium.

Pemba colors often correspond to the colors associated with the Orixás or spirits. For example, one might use red for Ogum and Exu, blue for Iemanjá, black for Omulu and Exu, purple for the Ibêji, green for Oxóssi and Ossãe, yellow for Iansã and Oxóssi, and pink for the intellectual spirits of the Oriental line.

SIGILS

As you just learned, the symbolic drawings that are made with the chalk are designed to invoke entities and bring them to earth. Once the spirits manifest, they draw their own symbols through the chalk held in the medium's hand in order to identify themselves. These sigils[11] are believed to possess an astral life of their own in that they carry part of the medium's and/or the spirit entity's consciousness. In this sense, although the markings involve symbols, they are not considered so much symbolic as actual. The drawings are part of the medium or the divinity, not just a representation of it. An entity may choose to draw one of the symbols by which it is typically recognized, or use something entirely different.

The groups of signs have their origins in many sources including Gnostic, Semitic, and ancient Egyptian, Aryan, African, and Amerindian traditions. They also include unique signs that are attributed to specific entities. Typical symbols include circles, hearts, crosses, sticks, arrows (drawn either straight, curved, or wiggly), lines, triangles, and hexagrams. The color will show either the Orixá or the line to which the entity belongs. If the "message" is coming from an entity, the medium interprets the signs according to the entity's explanation. In order to design an invocation sigil, the medium must study the meanings of countless symbols and memorize the personal sigils for each entity to be invoked. Some examples are illustrated in Figures 3 and 4 on the following pages.

AN ALTAR CLOTH OF OXALÁ.
This cloth shows one of the
invocational symbols for
the father of the Orixás.

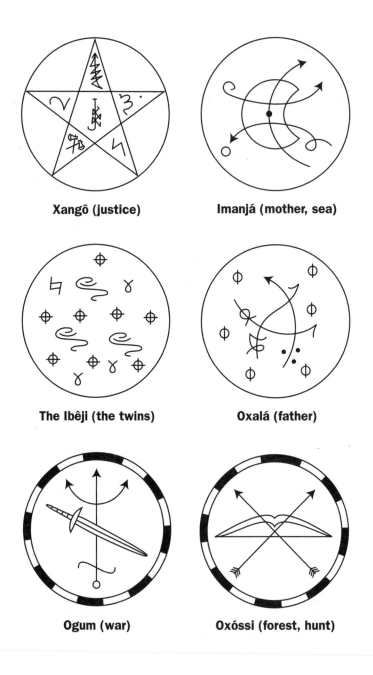

Figure 3: Examples of personal sigils used for invoking the Orixás.

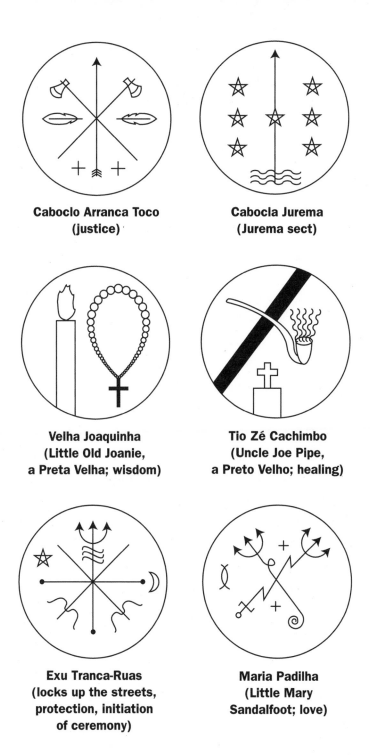

Caboclo Arranca Toco
(justice)

Cabocla Jurema
(Jurema sect)

Velha Joaquinha
(Little Old Joanie,
a Preta Velha; wisdom)

Tio Zé Cachimbo
(Uncle Joe Pipe,
a Preto Velho; healing)

Exu Tranca-Ruas
(locks up the streets,
protection, initiation
of ceremony)

Maria Padilha
(Little Mary
Sandalfoot; love)

Figure 4: More personal sigils for invoking the Orixás.

GUIAS

Another essential aid to mediumship are the *guias*[12] or "guides" that mediums wear while in trance. A guia is a long necklace with one to sixteen strands worn separately or attached at the back of the neck with a clasp. The strands are composed of colored glass or ceramic beads and sometimes shells, beans, nuts, and bark. The colors are associated with the spiritual entities that are incorporated, and vary according to the tradition. A list of bead colors appears in Appendix B under the descriptions of each Orixá. The guias for the Pretos Velhos are black and white, which shows equilibrium. The Caboclos use all the colors, which indicates that they manifest the powers of all the Orixás.

A guia serves as a link between medium and entity. This link is forged by the color or colors of the beads, which, it is believed, radiate the same energy as the entity. Whenever a medium wears the beads of his/her head Orixá, the response between them is strengthened.

Depending on the sect, mediums will wear only the beads of their head Orixás, while others use those of any entity they wish to incorporate or that protects or descends into their temple. Still others wear the beads of all the Orixás because these symbolize the line of the Caboclos.

No one may touch a set of beads except its owner once it is consecrated. It is recommended that the owners string the necklaces themselves to bring them even closer to their gods. Once the beads are purchased, the owner keeps them in a brand-new white box along with the herbs of the entity they represent. Then the beads are strung on nylon or steel thread and fixed with a clasp. The guias are consecrated in a special "washing" ceremony called an *amaci* (see Chapter 6), which is repeated once a year to remove any negativity that they may have accumulated. Many of the botanicals listed in Appendix C are used in washing ceremonies.

Here is a description of a washing ceremony written by José Ribeiro:[13]

> On the appointed day, all the members of the terreiro gather together dressed in white garments. A brand-new basin is set in the peji under one of Oxalá's alás,[14] illuminated by candles. No outsider is allowed to gain admittance while the ceremony is taking place. Everybody stands around the basin. Seven virgins[15] begin to crush the herbs to the sound of the other participants' clapping and singing. [When the herbs of the appropriate Orixás have been crushed and water is added to the bowl] each member comes forward and washes his/her beads in the basin. After concluding their amaci bath, the beads are taken out of the bowl and kept in a special place in the peji. The residual from the amaci bath is dispersed in running water, or the sea when the current is going out, taking with it the negativity the guias have attracted during the year. Later the spiritual leader rinses each set of beads with the incense of the appropriate Orixá, and returns the necklaces to their owners.

LINES AND LEGIONS

Throughout this book, many references have been made to "lines" and "legions" of Orixás and other entities. The lines exist in most Umbanda, Macumba and Quimbanda, and Candomblé sects, and in many Spiritist and Amerindian-style religions.

The lines represent vibrations that are believed to radiate through the cosmos. It is believed that everything in the universe vibrates at a specific rate. Each of the principal Orixás represents a vibrational line of one of the elements, for example, Iemanjá for water or Iansã for wind.

It is believed that one can contact and attract these vibrations by surrounding oneself with items that radiate the same sorts of energies that flow from the Orixás. This is why incenses, perfumes, prayers, invocations, botanicals, colors, drumbeats, and the like are used in ritual. Much care is taken to accumulate the "right" objects, and the rites are followed in the correct sequence at the proper time. Observing the ritual to the letter ensures that the desired potencies will manifest.

This idea is not at all foreign to practitioners of the Western Magickal Mystery Tradition. For instance, Ceremonial Magicians base their rituals on the research of eighteenth- and nineteenth-century magi, who in turn, culled their information from far earlier sources, including early civilizations of northern Africa, such as the Egyptians. In that belief system, the notion of the Doctrine of Signatures is paramount. This doctrine states that everything in the universe radiates particular frequencies and that like vibrations attract other like vibrations, called correspondences. So the Western Magician likewise surrounds him/herself with incenses, perfumes, colors, and the like that correspond to certain vibrations, in order to harness these energies and bring about changes in consciousness, or if you prefer, perform magick. (Several lines of Umbanda have been influenced by Western magick and include many of the same correspondences in their rites. One difference is that of emphasis. For example, the Western Magician may give importance to the influence of the planets, while the Umbandists focus more on the irradiations of the Orixás.)

Many lines of Umbanda exist. Usually sects will recognize seven, probably because seven is considered the mystical number in magick. Different terreiros follow different lines; practitioners do not entirely agree on which Orixás control which lines, and even what the seven lines should be. You can see how details such as the colors and other characteristics of the Orixás' attire, and days of the week on which to worship them, can easily lead to confusion. (One must remember that

with the exception of Candomblé and Amerindian faiths these religions are relatively new, and they are all based on oral traditions.
Nobody wrote about any of them until around the turn of the twenti-
eth century, and none of these religions was considered legal until
after mid-century. Even writers on Umbanda, one of the newest sects,
did not start publishing widely until the 1960s. No wonder there is
confusion about precepts and beliefs.)

Seven great Orixás control each line. Yet in the same way that
Olórun delegates his authority to his lieutenants, the Orixás who head
the lines give the task of directly ruling the world to entities who are
less spiritually evolved than they are, but who are on a higher level
than humans. These lieutenants and sub-lieutenants command
legions, also known as phalanxes. They, in turn, subdivide their
regimes, which are run by their underlings. Many of these entities are
Caboclos, Pretos Velhos, Exus, and Pombas-Giras. So you have seven
lines that are divided into seven legions. Each legion can be subdivided by seven almost into infinity.

The ruling entities proliferate almost endlessly within this great
astral administration by multiples of seven on three planes. These
three planes consist of intermediary Orixás, who number 2,793;
guides, who amount to 16,807; and protectors, who count 6,705,993 in
their ranks. According to Vera Braga de Souza Gomes,[16] the 6,705,993
can be multiplied by seven twice more to render overseers for every
aspect of human and earthly conditions. This amazing proliferation
reflects Brazilians' affinity for hierarchy and the belief that the more
minutely organized a structure, the more efficient it will become.

You can surely enjoy and even participate in these sects without
knowing the details about each and every line, legion, and legion sub-
division. It is enough for the layperson to know that when cult members talk of these things they are referring to evolved spirits who work
for the Orixás and who can be contacted directly. No one believes that

the great Orixás actually descend into the terreiro, because they are above human concerns. The entity that a medium contacts represents some minute portion of the Orixá's vibration. This is why Iansã, for example, can descend into myriads of terreiros at the same time. What you see is not her, but only a part of her.

For those who may be interested, here are some examples of lines and what they represent:

Oxalá—Considered the most powerful line, its practitioners practice positive magick and claim to diminish the intensity of the negativity produced by the legions of evil. They remove the "stain" of black magick spells. This line includes the legions of all the saints.

Iemanjá—This line protects women, travelers, and sailors, and counteracts Quimbanda spells that have been cast with the element water. It includes the legions of the Mermaids (led by Oxum), Undines (governed by Nanã), ocean and river Caboclas, sailors, and the Guiding Star.

Xangô—The followers of this line practice charity and spells for justice, and neutralize black magick. The line counts in its numbers the legions of Iansã as well as some Caboclos and Pretos Velhos.

Oxóssi—These adherents rely on folk medicine and *passes* (see Chapter 6) to cure people and animals of physical and psychic diseases. They also practice mediumship and unravel vengeance spells. The line houses most of the legions of Caboclos.

Orient—The followers incorporate spirits of Oriental magi and distinguished Incas, Aztecs, Arabs, Greeks, Romans, Egyptians, doctors, writers, philosophers, and scientists. The spirits help their adherents gain a general knowledge of all the occult sciences. The practitioners perform acts of charity and communicate to clients ways for curing their ills that have not yet been provided by science to humanity, but which they have learned from the wise spirits they worship.

Ogum—This line works in the realm of struggles, disputes, war, and vengeance according to the specific vibration of each legion. The line includes legions of Oguns with various second names, for example, Seaside Ogum, whom you met earlier in this chapter.

African—This line performs white magick and annihilates Quimbanda spells. The tradition invokes spirits of elders of many ancient African tribes as well as Pretos Velhos.

Some sects substitute other lines. For example, Esoteric Umbanda is strongly influenced by the Qabala and the Western Magickal Mystery Tradition. Understanding its precepts requires much study and remains beyond the reach of the masses. Popular Umbanda, on the other hand, embraces simpler themes and rituals that are more accessible to the people.

Carioca Umbanda is practiced mainly in the adjoining states of Rio de Janeiro, Espirito Santo, and Minas Gerais. It shows strong African and Indian influences built on a Spiritist base.

The purely Spiritist Line of Umbanda has followers mostly from the cities of Rio and São Paulo, and stays closer to Kardec's principles with some Afro-Indian influenced mixed in. A similar line is the White Line of Umbanda, which has removed the more controversial aspects of African influences such as blood initiations, animal sacrifices, and colorful clothing from their rituals.

The Line of the Souls is a tradition of Bantu origin that cultivates this nation's African ancestors. It also adapts many Qabalistic principles from the North of Africa. In Quimbanda, it is the line governed by Omulu, whose worshippers work in cemeteries.

The Exu Line exists both in Umbanda and Quimbanda, where it takes the place of the Oriental Line. This is because the Exus are considered to have a great deal of wisdom to impart. (This is one reason the Exus were invoked in the rite at the beginning of Chapter 3.)

Within Umbanda, there is even a Quimbanda line that practices Witchcraft. It is called "The Black Line" in opposition to "The White Line" of Oxalá.

There are some distinct Caboclo lines, which lean heavily on Amerindian traditions. The Aiahuasca Line is one of these. Its adherents in the north of the country eat a hallucinogenic plant that facilitates the trance state.

Quimbanda Lines

According to the *Dictionary of Afro-Brazilian Cults*,[17] standard Quimbanda lines include:

1. Line of the Souls—headed by Omulu.
2. Skeleton Line—headed by John Skeleton
   or Ogum of the Cemetery
3. Nagô Line—headed by Gererê.
4. Malei or Exu Line—headed by King Exu.
5. Mosurabi Line—headed by Caminoá.
6. Quimbanda Caboclo Line—headed by Black Panther.
7. Mixed Line—headed by Exu of the Countryside or Obaluaiê.

If all these variations seem confusing, the reader is in good company. Fernandes Portugal, who has studied, practiced, and ultimately written about the power of the Afro-Brazilian religions, claims that "the African-Indian-Catholic-Kardecist combinations in Brazil represent one of the most curious examples of religious syncretism in the entire world."[18]

O JOGO DE BÚZIOS: THE SHELL GAME

The young couple bent their thin frames awkwardly as they stooped to enter and sit on the floor of the tiny cubicle. Pai Efraim waited in cross-legged meditation to prepare himself in mind and spirit to throw the cowrie shells and receive the words of wisdom from Ifá. In a gesture of respect, the man removed his leather cowboy hat, and Pai Efraim could see that João's deeply bronzed face was still streaked with dust from working out on the range. His wife held their tiny, mewing baby to her flaccid breasts, which were loosely covered by a torn calico dress. She rocked the infant gently to comfort either it or herself, or perhaps both of them. Rosa had never before seen Pai Efraim dressed in his Chinese robe. The rich, flowing silk garment printed with circles made up of strange markings; the unfamiliar, acrid odor of the incense that puffed up in rings from the burner next to them; and Pai Efraim's serious demeanor all made her uneasy.

Then the Babalorixá smiled and softly patted the baby on the head. All was right again. "Boy or girl?" he asked in a gentle voice.

"Girl," Rosa answered.

"When was she born?"

"Just three days ago," João put in. "I was still out rounding up some of Seu Eufrázio's stray cattle." He gestured toward the baby and permitted himself a shy smile. "A fine surprise I found when I got home this morning."

The Babalorixá nodded in approval. "It is good that you have come to me as soon as possible so we can determine your newborn's future. Please sit quietly now, and do not be afraid of my words or gestures. What I do will ensure that Ifá will listen to us and communicate the will of Olórun."

João and Rosa held their breath and fixed their eyes on the holy man as he sprinkled more incense on the coals, picked up the pile of cowrie shells from the floor in his cupped hands, and closed his eyes. Soon in a sing-song voice, he began to intone the syllables of a language that was not Portuguese, but from what the couple could understand, included some names of the sainted Orixás.

> *Ogum nhe patakori, Ogum gessi gessi, meta,
> meta. Odô feiabá Iemanjá. Ora ieiê ô Oxum.
> Atotô Omulu. Ajuberu. Arô Bobói Oxumarê.
> Eparrei Iansã. Okê Arô, Okê Caboclo. Euê Ossãe.
> Obaniché, Kauô cabiecilê Xangô. Epa epâ Babá.
> Laroiê Exu Tranca-Ruas, Exu de Luz, Maria
> Padilha.* [19]

Then Pai Efraim, with his cupped hands still holding the shells, touched the forehead, swaddled chest, and fat little hands of the baby to put her in contact with the divinity. He made the sign of a cross over the white cloth on the floor and let the cowries drop from his hands and fall where they might.

After the clattering of the cowrie shells, the ensuing silence seemed even more complete. Rosa dared not exhale for fear of making a noise. Even the baby quieted down as if in anticipation of her destiny.

João swallowed hard once to clear his parched throat, and turned his gaze toward the shells scattered haphazardly in the circle on the floor. The circle was shaped from colorful strands of guias that kept the shells from straying from the cloth. João noticed that the cowrie shells had been cracked on one side so that depending on how they landed, they either showed their smooth, humped, polished backside or revealed a little bone-like structure that peeped through the open side. João also noticed that other objects lay in the circle, including a couple of seeds, nuts, and little stones.

"*Etalá Metalá!*" Pai Efraim's voice shattered the silence, making João and Rosa start. "Nanã is speaking, our ancient Lady of the Souls and of Impossibilities."

The parents leaned forward, tense, but silent, because they did not want to break the Babalorixá's line of communication with the Orixá.

He continued, "The configuration of this *odu* indicates that your little girl will be intelligent, thoughtful, and quiet. She will acquire much knowledge through her astute powers of observation, but she will also pass through many trials and experience terrible dissatisfaction in love. Yet with the exception of that one sphere of activity, she will conquer her troubles.

"She will grow to be a hard-working, honest girl, and very strong-willed. She will care for you throughout your old age. If you can try to understand her shattered love life and learn not to judge her in this, she will appreciate your sympathy and find great solace in your parental affection.

"Because she was born on a Saturday, she is also Iemanjá's child. Two powerful Orixás, the mother and the grandmother of the gods, watch over her. In good time, and as you can afford it, you should make sacrifices to all the Orixás to ensure the child's destiny."

After the grateful parents left with their infant in arms, the Babalorixá Pai Efraim, fatigued from the effort put forth in divination, knelt by the circle, lit a candle, and prayed to Ifá and Iemanjá:

> *Thank you for all that you have done for me, for*
> *the help that through you I have been able to give*
> *to those who came to me in need today. May I*
> *always see true and never lie. May I never deceive*
> *those who need me. Iemanjá, mother of mothers*
> *and my guardian and protectress, and Ifá, master*
> *of the ineffable, may you both always help me to*

understand the truths communicated to me. May I
never fail to fulfill my own destiny, which is to help
others. Amen.[20]

▲ ▲ ▲

As presented in the story above, one of the reasons people ask to have the cowrie shells thrown is to determine their guiding Orixás and their overall destinies. The game may also be played for many other reasons. For example, a client may want to know if an offering has been accepted by an Orixá, or he/she may desire the answer to a personal question. A spiritual leader may wish to know if a candidate for mediumship should be accepted into a terreiro, and if so, who will be his/her head Orixá.

Many types of divination are practiced by members of the Afro-Brazilian sects. Diviners may throw cut halves of an onion, called *alubaça*, to answer yes/no questions. They may toss four cola nuts (called *obi*), or perhaps divine with the dendê nut necklace called the *Opelé de Ifá* (Ifá's rosary). However, the *jogo de búzios*, the "cowrie shell game," is the most popular and complete form of divination.

At one time this game was reserved exclusively for Babalaôs, who were also priests of Ifá, the Orixá of divination, sometimes syncretized with the Holy Ghost. In contemporary Brazil, the old-time Babalaôs have all but disappeared, and Babalorixás and even other terreiro notables have taken up the gauntlet of communication with the ineffable spirit.

The game is complex, and since it mainly relies on oral tradition to interpret the meanings of the throws, it takes a dedicated student to become proficient at it. The game is played by throwing sixteen cowrie shells[21] into a circle that is either painted on the floor, on a special low table, or on a piece of cloth. The circle can also be made up of guias.

The shells are cracked open with a metal file or a screwdriver so that when they land, some show the cracked opening and others show the smooth, closed backs. The proportion of closed to open shells gives a number that is called an odu. Other interpretation factors include the relative positions of each shell and the configuration of the clumps into which they fall.

As noted in the scene above, sometimes the circle is ringed with guias that represent the Orixás. The circle can also hold objects such as stones, seeds, and coins, all of which modify the meaning of the spread. At other times, the diviner may lay a cloth that is covered with pontos riscados (sigils), which add even more meanings depending on where the shells fall. The particular head Orixá and other protectors of the client also determine the outcome of the interpretation.

Each shell represents a general topic such as alienation, tranquility, doubt, and insubordination. These topics can be interpreted in groups of four or singly. The shells may also be thrown two or three times to shed more light on the question. Every odu represents an Orixá, who "speaks" through it. For example, if sixteen shells are thrown, as in the story above, and thirteen land face up (open) with three face down (closed), the configuration shows an odu governed by the Orixá Nanã. The diviner needs to know the dominions of all the Orixás as well as their legends that illustrate the meanings of the odus, so that they may shed light on the question. They also must memorize specific "indications," or remedies, to overcome the negative aspects of the odu.

The odus can be subdivided several times by multiplying them by sixteen and taking the sum and multiplying it again by sixteen. This procedure renders 256 odus, which is considered a reasonable number for an expert reader to memorize. However, these odus can be multiplied again to add up to 4,096, each with its own fable and remedy. It is doubtful that anyone has ever memorized the more than 4,000 possible odus.

If the truth be told, many diviners rely on their intuitions more than memories to derive their interpretations. Speaking for one who has witnessed many Western modes of divination in action, I can say that no matter how the shell game is worked, its complexity makes methods such as rune casting look like child's play.

(For those who wish to pursue the study of the cowrie shells in divination, I refer you to my forthcoming book *The Shell Game*, to be published by Technicians of the Sacred, Burbank, California. It will be the only book I know of in English devoted entirely to this venerable Afro-Brazilian tradition.)

▲ ▲ ▲

Now that you have a background for understanding some of the practices of these sects, it is time to explore in the next chapter how to apply Brazilian magick to the healing of body and spirit.

NOTES

1. This ritual is adapted from Mestre Itaoman, *Pemba: A Grafia Sagrada dos Orixás* (Brasília: Thesaurus, 1990), 199–200.

2. See Appendix D for the ingredients of this and all the other Afro-Brazilian dishes and drinks mentioned in the spells in this chapter.

3. Mário César Barcellos, *Os Orixás e o Segredo da Vida: Lógica, Mitologia e Ecologia* (Rio de Janeiro: Pallas, 1991), 23.

4. Courtney Willis, one of the foremost authorities on African religions and head of Technicians of the Sacred, has created a list of botanical substitutes for animal sacrifices that he has based on his many years of research in the field. Write him in care of Technicians of the Sacred, 1317 North San Fernando Blvd., Suite 310, Burbank, CA 95104. Be sure to include a self-addressed, stamped envelope for a reply.

5. A variety of specific rites in Portuguese are categorized under the umbrella English term "spell." A *feitiço* is an object that has been instilled with a force to make it a powerful talisman and/or a force of good or evil. A *patuá* is an Indian term for an amulet that is instilled with a protective force and hung around the neck. An *encanto* is an enchantment or spell with the same purpose and executed in very much the same way as a spell in the Western Magickal Mystery Tradition. A *despacho* traditionally is an offering made to Exu or Pomba-Gira, but popularly, the term is used to indicate an offering to any entity in order to receive a boon. A *trabalho* is literally a "work," that is, a magickal working or spell to achieve a positive or negative effect. It often relies on Sympathetic Magick—fingernails, hair, personal clothing or objects, botanicals, candles, poppets, prayers, invocations, alimentary offerings—to cajole the entities to do one's bidding and to serve as a link between the entity, the petitioner, and the object that the petitioner wants to influence.

6. José Ribeiro, *O Jogo dos Búzios e as Cerimônias Esotéricas dos Cultos Afro-Brasileiros*, 6th ed. (Rio de Janeiro: Pallas, 1990), 58.

7. Adapted from Itaoman, *Pemba: A Grafia Sagrada dos Orixás*, 266–267.

8. The word in Portuguese is *ronda*, and refers to the legion of spiritual entities who keep evil entities from entering into the terreiro during a ceremony. It also refers to the circle of mediums who maintain "spiritual order" while a session is taking place.

9. This prayer is beautiful and elegant in its simplicity, and reminds me of the medieval Portuguese *cantigas*, or sung poetry—some of the best works, in my opinion, to come out of Portuguese literature. For the Portuguese speaker, here is the original text:

> *Oxalá, meu pai!*
> *Tem pena de mim, tem dó!*
> *Se a ronda do mundo é grande,*
> *O seu poder ainda é maior!*

10. Altair Pinto, *Dicionário da Umbanda*, 3rd ed. (Rio de Janeiro: Editora Eco, n.d.), 152.

11. Sigils are called *pontos riscados* (that is "scratched points" in Portuguese), because these points of contact with the spirit world are scratched on the ground either by a medium while in trance, or by any spellworker who wishes to invoke an entity.

12. The term in Portuguese is *guia* or *guiame*. They are not to be confused with the guias, who are spirit entities that accompany the medium while in trance and throughout his/her spiritual development.

13. José Ribeiro, *Cerimônias da Umbanda e do Candomblé*, 2nd ed. (Rio de Janeiro: Editora Eco, 1974), 85–86.

14. An *alá* is a white cloth canopy set over the altar.

15. This follows an old African custom, which is said to still take place on that continent.

16. Vera Braga de Souza Gomes, *O Ritual da Umbanda: Fundamentos Esotericos* (Rio de Janeiro: Editora Technoprint, 1989), 101.

17. Olga Gudolle Cacciatore, *Diconário de Cultos Afro-Brasileiros* (Rio de Janeiro: Forense Universitária/SEEC, 1977), 170.

18. Fernandes Portugal, *Axé: Poder dos Deuses Africanos* (Rio de Janeiro: Editora Eco, n.d.), 61.

19. Ogã Gimbereuá, *Ebós: Feitiços no Candomblê*, 5th ed. (Rio de Janeiro: Editora Eco, n.d.), 90.

20. Ibid., 103.

21. Some diviners like to throw four, eight, or seventeen shells or more, depending on his/her degree of expertise and inclination.

CHAPTER 6

HEALING

Once when living in Brazil, I came down with an inexplicable skin rash that looked like I'd been host to a legion of bull mosquitoes. The first "bite" appeared on my toe, and over the period of three weeks, the welts moved upward over my body, finally ending at the top of my head. I checked the bedding for bugs and boiled the sheets to no avail. The nurse at the American Consulate was at a loss for what to prescribe.

One day, Irma, a friend of the family with whom I was staying, came to visit. A recently initiated medium in the Umbanda tradition, she needed to borrow a white blouse to have

139

her picture taken for the official laminated card that showed her centro affiliation and the entities she could incorporate. Her primary entity was a Preto Velho named Zé da Mata (Forest Joe).

We went into the bedroom to find an appropriate blouse, and as we chatted, Irma noticed my bites and asked about them. She said she thought her Preto Velho might be able to help. All she required was a certain kind of pipe tobacco, a glass of water with coarse ground sea salt mixed in, and a brand-new square of white cloth to be able to manifest him. My friend and I agreed to help her with the experiment.

Irma nipped out to the local tobacco store as we prepared the water and found a suitable piece of material. When Irma returned we retreated to the bedroom. She told us that she was really only supposed to incorporate at the centro but since it was impossible at the time, she would bend the rules. She plopped down on the bed, placed the glass of water on the floor, and began to chant a simple prayer.

After a few minutes, her irises glazed over, and she stared upward so that almost all we could see were the whites of her eyes. She groaned softly, and lay back on the pillows.

After a moment, she straightened up and began to speak in a melodious tone with a gentle, old-fashioned accent, just like a slave of the last century. Zé da Mata had taken possession of Irma's body.

He asked for his pipe, which we filled with tobacco, lighted, and placed in his hand. He puffed on the pipe slowly until the tobacco smoldered like a miniature steam engine. I told him about my malady, and he drew on his pipe, deep in thought. After a short silence, he began to tell me in a soft voice that my problem stemmed from nervousness engendered by fluids from elemental spirits that had been attracted to my aura.

Humbly, he requested that I stand on the cloth. He got off the bed and began to blow smoke from his pipe at me—in my face, then down the front of my body to my feet, and behind me from head to toe.

Returning to face me, he used his free hand to make a waving motion around my head as if he were drawing something from the air around me. He worked his way down my body—front side, then back side—but never once touched me.

Finally, he gave me some words of advice about how to eliminate stress from my life, then he returned to the bed. One last time he inhaled on his pipe, and asked us to join him in a prayer of thanksgiving. Soon the medium blinked her eyes, and the Preto Velho vanished from her body. Irma was out of her trance.

We poured the water on the ground outside by the patio, and washed the cloth in the sink. From that day forward I never contracted another "bite," and the old ones soon lost their itch and eventually disappeared. So ended the first, and to me, not the least of many impressive healing demonstrations I was to witness among the Afro-Brazilian sects.

In this chapter you will again meet the Caboclos and Pretos Velhos of the Brazilian pantheon and see how the people rely on them to cure physical and psychological ailments. You will also learn how Brazil's great natural tropical pharmacy is used in folk medicine and magick.

SOME THEORIES ABOUT DISEASE

In the Afro-Brazilian magickal system, it is believed that everything in the universe is continually being exposed to the action of different energies. Some of these energies have been identified by science, and include gamma rays and the auras of animals and plants. Others, given our lack of scientific sophistication, have not yet been identified. Practitioners claim that some of these emanations, known as fluids, are so subtle yet powerful that they can bend or break physical objects. They range in density from the most etheric and spiritual to the almost physical. Human beings, who form part of the universe, naturally emit an exudate that we call the human aura. Some healers, known as aura readers, can perceive these human exudations and evaluate a patient's physical and mental condition based on the aura's size, shape, and color. In this sense, aura healing in Brazil closely parallels the Western Magickal Mystery Tradition.

However, there the similarity ends. In the creed of Afro-Brazilian sects, some disease is caused by corrupt fluids emitted from putrescent plants and animals and from astral entities of a low order of development, such as the elementals and unevolved spirits of the dead. These noxious disturbances can impregnate the aura with physical or psychological illnesses. They can also infiltrate the atmospheres of a house, store, vehicle, outdoor space, or even a terreiro. Harmful fluids can be expelled or "discharged" (as the term translates literally from Portuguese) directly on the astral level by evolved entities such as the Pretos Velhos and Caboclos, the Orixás, or by one's own holy guardian angel.

Often the fluids are discharged in special rituals by the medium through which the entities speak. During these rites, the medium will render a vegetable and sometimes an animal offering; purify the patient with salt and water, incense, and/or herbal baths; charge a talisman or amulet and lay on hands; and most importantly, will offer prayers. In the ceremony described at the beginning of this chapter, the spirit of the Preto Velho, one of the most revered spirit healers, communicated through the medium by using tobacco smoke, salt and water, and laying on hands in a process called a *passe*—a pass. In this procedure, healing energy is sent through the hands while the medium passes his/her hands around the patient's aura without touching the body.

THE EVIL EYE

Another principal cause of sickness, trouble, and woe according to the Afro-Brazilian belief system is the "evil eye." It is held that both positive and negative fluids accumulate inside a person based on his/her actions throughout this lifetime and past incarnations. Some people amass an overabundance of positive energy, which they can direct toward healing others by using the power of the will. Others store negativity, and like a snake that builds up venom in its pouch, discharge it from time to time, harming other people or creating treacherous environments. Malefic energy is thought to flow from the eyes, thereby confirming the popular expression that the eyes are indeed the windows to the soul.

Like a psychic vampire, the person cursed with the evil eye may have no knowledge of it, and is often appalled to learn that he/she is causing trouble. Occasionally, out of horror and remorse, the afflicted one may turn the eye inward and cause great self-inflicted bodily harm. Besides observing the horror created by these infelicitous souls, a trained medium can identify the responsible parties by reading their auras, which appear carmine-tinged. In fact, it is said that one way to deflect the evil eye is to wear red clothing; because "like attracts like," the venom will stick to the clothes, not to the person wearing them.

Through ritual, a medium can rid a person of the evil eye, obsessed spirits, and resultant infections, as long as the cause of the malady is not karmic. The following rite also works to cleanse the general environment of this kind of negativity, as well as the place where the victim lives.

Take a broom made of garlic straw in one hand and a glass of salt-water in the other. With the water in your left hand and the broom in your right, start sweeping from the back of the house to the front door. Leave the water outside the door to be disposed of later in the ground.

Return to the house and light a white candle inside the entryway and an oil lamp in the most sacred place in the house (such as the occupant's personal altar or in the bedroom). Light purification incense and cense each room of the house thoroughly. To close the ritual, extinguish the flame of the burning candle. Repeat the rite every day for three or seven days until the house feels purified.

When leaving the house, repeat the following prayer:

> *I..., covered with the mantle of Oxalá, will be saved from the evil eye, from envy, jealous hatred, and all malefic energies. I will walk everywhere without fear, for I know I will always be under the protection of the Archangel Gabriel.*
>
> *May the arm of Zambi restrain whosoever wishes to do me harm. May my enemies be paralyzed whenever they harbor evil thoughts against this sinning son/daughter. So mote it be!* [1]

Other ways to counteract the evil eye consist of amulets and offerings, which will be described later in this chapter.

HORARY HEALING

In horary healing— healing by the hours of the day and night—psychic healers practice their rites according to specific hours of the day or night because they believe that at certain times positive energy currents are strongest. This resembles the idea in the Western Magickal Mystery Tradition that certain rituals are best performed at dawn, noon, and sunset. Since Brazil lies close to the equator, little differentiation is seen between the hours the sun rises and sets in summer and winter. Therefore, Brazilians can more easily refer to a particular hour when a ceremony should be performed rather than counting the minutes of daylight and darkness in order to ascertain the proper time.

The hour of Oxalá is 6:00 A.M. (dawn), and this is the time recommended for prayer for the ill and afflicted. At noon, the hour of Ogum, when the sun shines most intensely, is an appropriate time to begin rituals to conquer obstacles and destroy evil. The "Spiritualist Humanity Hour" comes at 6:00 P.M., and is a good time to open dialogue with Zambi, and again pray for the ill and afflicted. Wherever an Umbandist is at this time of evening, he/she should stop for seven minutes and meditate on the astral current of positive energy in evidence at this hour. The most powerful spiritual and mental current is ascertained to occur around 8:00 P.M., which is when most group ritual work begins. Depending on the purpose of the session, it may start at 8:00, 8:20, 8:25, 8:27, or 8:30 P.M. Each minute number brings a particular influence drawn from the numerological system of the Western Magickal Mystery Tradition.

Healing sessions should end by around 10:00 P.M. so that everyone has a chance to get home before midnight, which is considered the "Zero Hour," or dead hour of the night, and is dedicated to Exu. This hour is considered so negative that if a session is going on at that time, all activity is suspended, and prayers are offered to carry the group beyond the midnight hour. Here is an example of a prayer for crossing the "Zero Hour":

> *Great Hour! ... Hour of silence. Hour of human respect for the unknown power.*
>
> *In every person's heart at this moment vibrates the flame of the most fervent and burning love for the All-Father.*
>
> *May the protection of Oxalá be spilled over onto Humanity!*

Twelve strokes mark the 'Great Hour.' Oxalá had twelve apostles when he came to this planet. Man must traverse twelve houses in his life on this planet. Twelve words exist in Umbanda for protection.

Zambi, my Father, give us your protection. Keep us safe from evil influences. Saravá!

Hour of Silence!

Hour of Pardon!

Hour of Repentance!

Great Hour!

Saravá to those who work Umbanda!

Saravá to the People of the Great Hour!

Saravá! [2]

HEALING WITH WATER

Many of the Orixás, especially the females, take their names from African bodies of water, as this element is associated with femininity. Water is important to the Afro-Brazilian traditions because of its therapeutic values. Also, it is considered an element fairly easy to magnetize with positive or negative charges. When it springs fresh from forest or waterfall, it is considered pure and unsullied. Water from *cataracts* (waterfalls) is used for purification baths in rituals of initiation and baptism. It helps fine-tune the medium's sensitivity, and keeps subevolved beings from attaching themselves to the aura.

The sea, too, is revered because its seemingly infinite waters provide fish, mollusks, seaweed, and other food, as well as salt, which is essential to sustaining human life. Brazil was settled by the Portuguese, who were a seafaring people and always strived to remain close to the ocean. This is why the majority of Brazilian cities and towns ring the coastline, and another reason the ocean plays an important part in Afro-Brazilian ritual. The salt in the water is believed to repel nefarious spirits and pernicious emanations.

Tap water also makes an excellent source for trapping negativity in the environment and therefore is used in purification rituals and almost any other kind of ceremony. Practitioners differ about the proper way to dispose of the contaminated liquid. Some say it should be poured down a sink drain with the water taps on full blast to dissolve the negativity. Others claim that defiled water may never be disposed of in the public water system, but should be drizzled on greenery, especially grass, so it can be reabsorbed into nature.

Here is a short spell you can perform using water: Caboclo Uytán's recipe for insomnia. To alleviate insomnia caused by obsessed or malefic spirits or negative thought forms, place a full glass of water on the patient's headboard before retiring. If the insomnia does not disappear immediately, look for a physical or karmic cause.

HEALING HERBS

Botanicals are considered so vital to working magick that no ceremony can be undertaken without the permission of Ossãe, the Orixá in charge of botanicals. Plant materials enter into every aspect of ritual, including healing. Each herb is believed to possess an etheric force easily capable of absorption by the skin. Every botanical crystallizes a particular virtue such as fertility, peace, vigor, protection, longevity, courage, happiness, good fortune, and glory, and may also drive away illness, negativity, misery, and noxious fluids. During germination and growth, plants absorb and store immense energies from the earth and sky. When a person ingests a medicinal botanical, the energy is freed and circulated throughout the body and into the aura. The herbal energy both adds something of its own nature and helps release the patient's own pent-up energy to stimulate self-healing.

Besides being the primary ingredients of folk medicine, botanicals are included in incenses, purification, and discharge baths, and amulets and talismans. The herbs of the Orixás are important in initiations because they help establish a magickal connection between Orixá and the medium.

PLANT SACRIFICES

The acolyte swathed in a white gown, encircled by other gossamer-clad initiates, kneels before the altar. A woman steps forward and covers her shoulders with the sacred *ojá*, a snowy shawl. Another places a white basin before her on the floor. Somewhere a voice breaks the silence with an incantation, and one by one, everyone joins in. As if mesmerized, the initiate sways slightly back and forth, letting her head drop over the bowl. Suddenly, the Ialorixá steps forward with a container brimming with a dark green liquid, and slowly drips it over the medium's head, the excess drops being absorbed by the ojá. The amaci (headwash) has strengthened the bond between the new initiate and her guiding Orixá, known as the Orixá of her head. Thus fortified, she is ready to work magick.

When an initiate prepares an herbal concoction, he/she is aware that a sacrifice is being made. The sap extracted from the pulp, made by grinding the herbs with a mortar and pestle and steeping them in cold water, represents the plant's life blood or fundamental energy. When this essence is poured over a person's body, it mixes its scent with human odor, and carries the smell away with it into the earth. It is believed that Mother Earth is aware of all odors and feeds off them. The mingling of human and plant odors creates a mini-sacrifice that appeases the earth and delays the time when the human body, decaying in death, will literally become fodder for the ground. All plant sacrifices are made under the auspices of Ossãe, the Forest Lord.

This concept of sacrifice, as you saw in Chapter 5, extends to animals as well. In the same way that practitioners of Afro-Brazilian religions sacrifice herbs, they may also render animal food offerings in order to maintain a balance between humans and nature for the well-being of all. For the believer, this respectful sacrificial rite helps keep the earth's cycles moving, and in the end, promotes life.

COLLECTING BOTANICALS

If ever you should find yourself journeying into the vast tropical forests of Brazil to gather herbs for healing or ritual purposes, Afro-Brazilian herbalists will advise you that you would do well to mind the following procedures. Always carry along a roll of tobacco and some honey to leave at the foot of a fig tree as an offering to Ossãe. Otherwise, it is possible that he will camouflage the plants you need, and you will return home empty-handed. Never enter the sacred forest when you are not in a state of purity. This means you will have to refrain from intercourse, smoking tobacco, or drinking alcohol for at least twenty-four hours prior to collecting herbs, and if you are a woman, you cannot gather or prepare botanicals when menstruating.

Be sure you know the Orixá to whom the herbs you are harvesting belong. Collecting botanicals from the wrong divinity at the wrong time, according to tradition, can have fatal consequences because you might incur the Orixás' wrath. From 6:00 A.M. to noon, harvest herbs associated with Oxalá and Nanã. From noon to 6:00 P.M., gather those herbs belonging to Ogum, Xangô, Oxum, and Iansã. The evening hours until midnight belong to the Exus, Pombas-Giras, and Omulu. The wee hours from midnight until 6:00 A.M. are right for gathering herbs of Oxóssi, Ossãe, and Iroco.

When preparing medicines, be sure to sing songs that celebrate the virtues and powers of each botanical. As a sign of respect for the botanical's axé, keep your back unclothed, and when you are done, exit the preparation area facing the herbs as if you were in the presence of a king.

Whether a botanical is used for magickal or curative purposes, the Orixá to whom it belongs, and when, how, and in what combination it is used, is a secret jealously guarded by the spiritual chiefs. However, information about some botanicals has managed to escape into the public domain. Appendix C names some of these botanicals, the Orixás with whom they are associated, and some common uses in healing and magick.

INCENSE

From the time he moved into the tiny one-bedroom apartment in Botafogo, Nelson's life skidded downhill. His girlfriend of five years suddenly left him, complaining that he was no fun anymore. He was reprimanded at the company where he worked as a salesman for having lost his edge. To soften the blow, his boss asked him to have his health checked because he appeared a bit "green around the gills."

If the truth be told, Nelson wasn't feeling at all up to snuff, and the more time he spent moping around the apartment the more depressed he became, especially when he worked in the *área*—the room off the kitchen where the maid washed laundry, beat out rugs, and performed other household chores. As was the custom in Brazil, a tiny maid's bedroom, really no more than a closet, was crammed in on one side of the área up against an even more miniscule bathroom. Since Nelson couldn't afford a maid, he did all the housework himself, and set up his woodworking bench in the maid's room to pursue his hobby building birdhouses.

But now he just couldn't seem to muster the energy to go into the maid's room and tinker around. Even performing daily chores in the área left him dizzy and trembling, and awash in an overwhelming feeling of self-pity.

Naturally, the doctors could find nothing wrong. They only told him to take a two-week vacation in the mountains. "Easy to say if you're a wealthy doctor!" he thought.

One Sunday, he managed to drag himself over to his sister's house for dinner. Maybe the activity of his four nieces playing around him and the lively conversation of his brother-in-law would lift his spirits. His family was shaken by his appearance, and it didn't help when his sister told him he looked like a desicated leaf. His brother-in-law, Gil, however, offered some constructive advice.

"Why don't you let the pai-de-santo from our terreiro visit you. Maybe he can suggest some herbs or something."

Gil's pai-de-santo, Seu Tomás,[3] was a portly, balding gentleman, full of life, and kind words. On his first visit he was drawn immediately to the área, where he set up a folding chair for himself, and put a glass of saltwater and a lighted candle on the ground in front of himself. After five minutes of meditation, he charged out into the kitchen and called triumphantly to Nelson.

"I have it! I know what the trouble is. You are being disturbed by the spirit of a maid who used to work here a long time ago and committed suicide right here in her bedroom. The poor soul still clings to the place, and is sapping your strength in order to exist."

Before a startled Nelson could utter a word, the medium disappeared with a promise to return the next day at noon to take care of the "little matter." Seu Tomás was as good as his word, and came back the following day with another glass of saltwater, a bag of loose incense, and two incense burners and coals. He placed the smaller burner on top of the coffee table, and set the larger one in the área, and lighted seven swift-lighting coals in it.

"Since she worked in every room in the house, I have to cense all the rooms, not just where she made passage from this life," he explained while deftly sifting some fragrant dried leaves and resins onto the red-hot coals.

Then he intoned an "Our Father" and three "Hail Marys" and set to work. Beginning at the back of the house, he censed it with the copious smoke that billowed up in fragrant clouds from the burner. He repeated the same procedure in each room. First he stood in the center, and with the burner held out in front of him, made a straight line to a corner of the room, then back to the center. He walked back and forth to each corner, then from the center of the room to the middle of each wall, censing all the while (see Figure 5). Throughout the ritual, he uttered the following prayer:

> *I purify this house, and everywhere I go with this*
> *incense burner, I free the environment of all visi-*
> *ble and invisible malignant currents. And so, by*
> *the grace of God, Nelson Vieira will be free of all*
> *danger in the Name of the Holy Trinity, Olórun,*
> *Oxalá, and Ifá. So mote it be.*

Seu Tomás finished at the front door, and then censed Nelson, first from head to toe in front, then again in back. He put the glass of water and the smoking burner outside in the hall. Nelson deeply breathed in

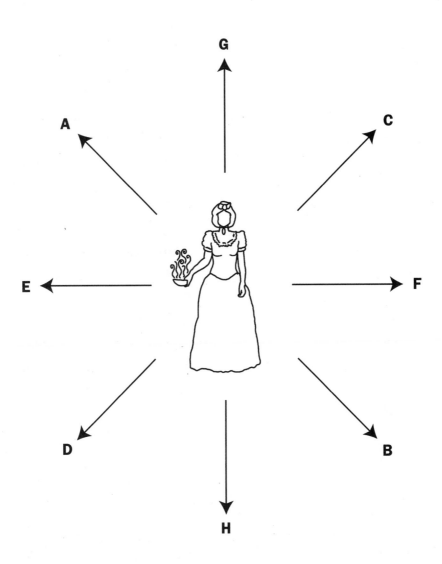

Figure 5: How to cense a room to drive away negative spirits.

the smoke as he was instructed. He felt a little giddy, but curiously refreshed.

The medium then lit a coal in the burner on the coffee table, sprinkled on sharper-smelling incense, and offered a prayer to Ogum. After the ceremony, he informed Nelson that the ritual was over, and he was free from the obsessed spirit of the maid. He refused any payment for the service, but suggested that Nelson make a donation to the terreiro for the price of the materials and another donation to Seu Tomás' head Orixá, Ogum, who would gratefully accept the remuneration.

As soon as the spiritual chief left, Nelson began to feel better. It was almost as if a great weight were lifted from his shoulders, and he felt relieved. His pace picked up, his girlfriend came back. Eventually they wed, and he received a bonus at the end of the year for selling more than anyone else in the company.

Out of curiosity, Nelson tried to find out if a suicidal maid had ever lived in the apartment. The former tenants knew nothing, but they said that they had moved because the place felt creepy. The landlord had not heard anything either, but he had owned the apartment for only fifteen years.

One day, Nelson's wife was talking to the little white-haired lady who lived down the hall, and the lady remembered the story as if it were yesterday. Back in the 1930s, a quiet, single man rented the apartment and, as was the custom in those days, hired a live-in maid. The poor creature was ugly as the hind end of a dog and she hated her life. But she had great ambitions, and told everyone that she would force her employer to marry her. When one fine day he announced his engagement to another woman, the maid fell into a deep depression. Early on the morning of the wedding, despairing in her bedroom, she took her own life. Her employer and his bride never returned to the apartment.

Function of Censing

Ridding houses and other environments and people of obsessed spirits and negative fluids is one function of censing. Afro-Brazilian shamans believe that perfume causes repercussions on the astral, mental, and spiritual planes. The aroma of burning incense releases the axé imprisoned in plants and attracts positive energy. It also aids mediumistic development by conditioning the mind to vibrations emitted by spirits, and helps cement the bond between the medium and his/her head Orixá. The art of burning incense brings into play three of the primary elements, as well as spirit. Earth is represented by the clay burner and the botanicals themselves, fire by combustion and flame, and air by smoke. Spirit entities are also attracted by the smoke. Place a glass of water next to the burner to capture emitted impurities, and all four elements, plus spirit, are represented.

Types of Incense

Individual tablets are prepared by initiates for laypersons to burn in the home, for the uninitiated are not supposed to use the loose kind. To burn the wrong incense on the wrong occasion invites negative elements to enter a person's sphere. One type of stick incense that is suitable for anyone to use is called Hana-Noka. This incense emits seven different perfumes that are said to be enjoyed by everyone. It is recommended that a person burn Hana-Noka in the home to attract love. It is also recommended for doctors' and dentists' offices and beauty salons, because the scent alleviates stress and creates an agreeable environment.

In the temple, different incenses are burned during general public sessions, rites of mediumistic development, initiation ceremonies, and as offerings to the Orixás. Exactly what constitutes the appropriate combination of scents to call upon each Orixá is a closely guarded secret, but some general indications of the Orixás to whom certain herbs belong, and therefore, presumably are burned, are indicated in Appendix C. In addition, the following list describes occasions, other than head-making and mediumistic development, when incenses are offered in petitions, the correct entities to whom they should be offered, and the purpose of the incense:

Exu—Purifies the terreiro and the environment when burned before beginning sessions on Mondays and Saturdays. Use before burning purification incense for any rite. Be sure to light separate coals.

Iansã—Makes females who wish to marry irresistible and connects them to Iansã, so she will find them a mate.

Ibêji—Helps children up to the age of fourteen with their studies or during illnesses.

Caboclos of Umbanda—Used to begin and end charity sessions; also suitable to burn in residences, vehicles, and business places.

Iemanjá—Protects travellers when burned before business trips or vacations; an excellent scent for brides; binds Umbanda spells.

Ogum—Eliminates obsessed spirits from heavily charged environments and people.

Ogum of the Forest—Physically protects policemen, soldiers, or anyone who holds a physically dangerous occupation.

Ogum of the Seashore—Invokes the Undines and mermaids; for terreiros located in seaside cities; protects sailors.

Oriental Spirits—Creates a high-minded, psychically balanced environment when burned at Spiritualist, Spiritist, and Umbandist meetings.

Oxalá—Opens sessions where the spiritual leader is a male; purifies business establishments (burn frankincense first).

Oxóssi—Protects those who work with the forest people.

Oxum—Brings good health, prosperity, and love, and brings harmony to the home.

Xangô—Benefits judges, lawyers, legislators, linguists, professors, translators, and writers (burn benzoin before and after in a different burner or on other coals).

Caboclos, Pretos Velhos, Exus, and Pombas-Giras also require tobacco so they can blow the smoke on patients to cure them of various maladies. Critics of this Macumba/Umbanda custom claim that indulgence in tobacco only perpetuates smoking as a vice. Adherents of these traditions counter that tobacco smoke, when used judiciously in rituals, cleanses and energizes. They say that outside the temple mediums usually do not indulge, and that to ban the practice of censing with tobacco would destroy an important link between medium and entity.

Caboclos and Pretos Velhos prefer pipes. Pretos Velhos sometimes mix their tobacco with lavender, cinnamon, rosemary, and rue. Caboclos may smoke weak cigars; the Exus, on the other hand, opt for the strongest brands; the Pombas-Giras favor fine cigarettes and cigarillos.

Common Censing Herbs

Generally, the herbs used in censing are of native Brazilian origin, but most of the resins hail from the Orient, which sect members consider the birthplace of spirituality. Common ingredients include:

benzoin gum—inspires the intellect and intuition.

coffee—repels negativity.

Brazilian storax—creates an atmosphere of peace and tranquility.

frankincense—confers the power of Oxalá.

garlic shells—repel negative fluids.

lavender—attracts women, repels men; harmonizes.

myrrh—purifies; is considered a scent of the Line of the Souls.

rosemary—attracts men, repels women; purifies.

rue—protects and purifies.

sandalwood—vibrates pure, divine energy.

A Song to Sing while Censing during Charity Sessions	▲	*Cense with Jurema's herbs!* *Cense with rue and Guinea pepper!* *Cense with Jurema's herbs!* *Cense with rue and Guinea pepper!* *Benzoin, rosemary and lavender,* *Let's all cense now, children of the Faith!*[4]

RITUAL BATHS

When I was living in Brazil and researching this topic, I was privileged to attend a closed session for mediumistic development. Before I could enter the sacred space, just like anyone else, I needed to be purified.

Two women led me to the back of the building where a small shower stall was located, and had me remove my clothes. Then from a clay jar, they spilled a mixture of water, oil, and fragrant herbs over my body from shoulders to toes, first down my front, then down my back. All the while, they chanted a melody in the Yoruba tongue. They dried me off, and censed me from top to bottom, front and back with sweet-smelling smoke.

Then they dressed me in a long, blue skirt and white lace blouse, tying a blue sash around my shoulders so that its ends hung down my back. They gave me a beautiful necklace of seashells and beads to wear, and wrapped a turban around my head, all in the style of the Iemanjá, whom they maintained was my protectress. I was now properly purified and prepared to participate in the secret rite (which unfortunately must remain a mystery to the uninitiated).

Abô Baths

Brazilians must rank among the cleanest people in the world. If they have water available, they may shower as many as three times a day. To me, it has always been one of life's little mysteries how they are able to keep all that white, 100-percent cotton clothing they wear—particularly in rituals—spotless and wrinkle-free.

Their attitude toward hygiene is reflected in their religion. Bathing forms as integral a part of Afro-Brazilian ritual as censing, and often acts as a support for the same purposes. The *abô*[5] bath is taken during initiation rites to cleanse the neophyte and prepare the sacred beaded necklace that the new medium will use to strengthen the link with the Orixá of his/her head. Abô baths are also given to any sacred object that will enter into rites, including the divinational cowrie shells, bracelets, knives, coins, clay pots, wooden spoons, and guias. Different kinds of water, including water from the sea, rivers, and waterfalls, are used for special purposes.

The precise recipes are often kept a mystery from all but the spiritual leaders, but many common herbs are listed in Appendix C. Often tinctures of benzoin, rosemary, lavender, frankincense, rue, myrrh, and Guinea pepper leaves are added to the bath according to the indications of one's spirit guides. Botanicals should never be boiled; instead, the water is heated, turned off, and the crushed herbs are allowed to steep in the covered pot before they are pressed through a sieve in a process called maceration. Often the botanicals are not even heated, but allowed to steep in cold water for twenty-four hours. In some Candomblé sects, the leftover botanicals are burned like incense in an earthen vessel.

Discharge Baths

Purification baths are called *banhos de descarga* ("discharge baths" in Portuguese) because they neutralize the charge from negative energies. These preparations, made from water, coarse-ground salt, herbs, and sometimes balms, are designed to rid a person, dwelling, locale, business, store, or animal of obsessed spirits and negative fluids in the same way as purification incense does. The mixtures also attract divine protection and defend a person against the evil eye.

Pre-packaged discharge baths can be bought by the layperson from casas de santo, the shops described in Chapter 1 that deal in Afro-Brazilian religious supplies (see pages 2–3). They are recommended for general psychic development, and help lift the spirits of a person who feels emotionally or physically downtrodden. They are suitable for someone who has never before experienced a discharge bath and who may attend a public rite in a temple, and for anyone who works in the law or has to deal with the public every day.

Amacis

A unique tradition is the amaci,[6] a special head bath meant to strengthen the tie between medium and his/her head Orixá, and fortify the medium's spirit so he/she can withstand repeated possessions and resist negative influences. Amacis are also used to bathe the paws and horns of sacrificed animals, and to purify ritual necklaces and other objects.

The water used in an amaci to "make the head" of a child of Xangô should come from a waterfall or a thunderstorm. Oxum's initiates must bathe in clear, natural spring water, and Iemanjá's followers in seafoam. Ogum's children need to collect water from a downpour.

The liquid must stand for seven days in a pitcher in the cell where the future initiate is sequestered. Then it is taken to the altar where a maceration of herbs is prepared from botanicals sacred to Ossãe and the future medium's head Orixá. During the initiation rite, this liquid, combined with blood from sacrificed animals and other materials, is poured over the person's head. The excess is soaked up by a towel that is secured around the acolyte's shoulders. Many mediums claim that they feel an electric charge run through their bodies at this point in the ritual.

The Popcorn Bath

One day I returned from work at the National Library to the house where I was staying with Brazilians to find that the entire inside of the dwelling was covered with popcorn. Chairs, lamps, tables, beds, floors—every flat surface brimmed with crunchy white popcorn. One of the women who lived in the house practiced Macumba, and her spirit guide had told her she was infected by the evil eye, contracted while she was in a trance performing healing. Her mãe-de-santo came and spread the hot sand-popped white corn, called Flowers of Omulu, around the house, advising her not to remove it for twenty-four hours, then to sweep it all away with a special broom.

Popcorn is a sacred food of Omulu, and is used in spells for healing and as an amulet. It is also a favorite food of other entities like Exu. Besides nullifying the evil eye, the popcorn bath can attract happiness and good fortune. In this case, the spiritual leader prays over the corn while it is being prepared, then secretly goes to the patient's home, and without anyone seeing, spreads it on the roof. The popcorn is never removed; it just disintegrates naturally.

A personal popcorn bath for better health is popped in a brand-new clay pan accompanied by prayers to Omulu for the welfare of the afflicted one. Then the patient stands on a brand-new white cloth to catch the popcorn that is spilled over him/her. After the bath, the healer collects the popcorn in the cloth and disposes of it in the earth.

AMULETS AND TALISMANS

Another healing technique shared by Afro-Brazilian sects as well as most other magickal mystery traditions involves charging and carrying amulets and talismans. The items that fall into this category can include anything believed to be of worth to the wearer. Some objects are thought to possess such high intrinsic value that they can be worn by anyone. All amulets and talismans must be magnetized (that is, activated by bathing them in an abô bath) and instilled with power through prayer. In this way, the objects remain potent for years.

In the Afro-Brazilian traditions, amulets protect the wearer by absorbing any negative energy with which the wearer may come in contact, even if this negative charge is emitted by the wearer him/herself. Typical amulets include a bulb of garlic, a handful of frankincense peas, a rue branch, or precious stones.

Talismans, on the other hand, both protect from evil and negativity and attract positive energy. Typical examples include a piece of paper drawn with the magickal sigil of the protecting entity, a Roman Catholic medal, a dried broadbean, or a kola nut.

The *figa* is one of the most famous examples of a talisman. Well respected throughout the Mediterranean countries and Brazil, it consists of an upward thrusting fist with the thumb protruding between the index and second fingers (see Figure 6). Although figas usually are carved from wood and stand about a foot high, all sizes exist. Silver and gold figa necklaces are prized. Sometimes other talismans, such as horseshoes and four-leafed clovers, are etched around the wrist

Figure 6: The figa.

of the figa. It is popularly believed that you should never buy a figa for yourself because its effectiveness will be adversely affected. This talisman must be given to you by someone else, or you need to steal it! If your figa is small enough, wear it as a necklace. If you acquire a large wooden figa, place it by your living room door to ward off intruders, or in your bedroom to keep obsessed spirits and the Eguns at bay.

Cowrie shells, which are used in divination, also compose the sacred necklaces of the Pretos Velhos and Caboclos, and are used to decorate some of the Orixás' costumes, as are sea shells. Starfish protect a residence or business, and bring prosperity. Seahorses can be charged as talismans for those who would try their luck at horseracing, gambling, and the lottery. According to Umbandists, Guinea pepper is one of the most efficacious talismans that exists, but it should only be used by those who know how, otherwise, its force can backfire.

Some sites are considered to possess high value as amulets and talismans. Sanctuaries, birthplaces of holy people, and churches fall into this category. Of course, the most sacred spaces of all, alleged to be surrounded by vibratory halos of pure love and light, are the terreiros.

PASSES

A principal reason laypeople attend open sessions and charity sessions at centros is to consult with entities who speak through mediums, and have healing performed. Before entering the ritual space, visitors check in at the directory and are assigned numbers for their consultations that begin soon after the mediums incorporate. One of the most popular kinds of healing performed by mediums is the passe, or laying on of hands without actually touching the patient's body. This is, in part, what Seu Tomás did earlier in this chapter to relieve Nelson of the disconsolate maid's spirit and what Zé da Mata did to help cure my bites.

In the Afro-Brazilian sects, it is believed that every human being has the capacity to focus healing energy from the universe, but that some are able to control and send more intense emanations than others. When a medium focuses this energy through an Orixá or other entity, he/she is called a healer medium. When able to transmit this energy without supernatural help, the person is known as a magnetizer. Both types are able to repair damage to tissues and organs through the energy transmitted by their hands. However, those who receive healing power from an entity are considered more powerful, because the energy that flows from just one entity is believed to be far more intense than that of several humans working together.

Skeptics wonder why healers cannot simply communicate this energy through an act of will in the same way Uri Geller bends spoons.[7] Healers respond that their arms and hands act like conducting wires that transmit electrical charges from the cosmos, and that they are only the vehicles of this healing energy.

In order to become the unsullied vessel for the perfect communication of this energy, a healer must refrain from smoking and drinking, eat a well-balanced diet, and be able to banish (at least for the period when the healing is taking place) any personal emotions such as pain, anger, jealousy, excitement, happiness, or disconsolation. Healers believe that prayer helps put them into the proper frame of mind and dissipates these emotional elements.

The body can fall into disequilibrium either through bombardment of negative fluids, or attachment of entities to the aura or physical disease. To rectify the imbalance, the medium attempts with the passe to realign the body's chakras so that a perfect vibratory harmony is reestablished between the chakras, the body's organs, and the vibration

of the cosmos. Although it is not necessary for a patient to believe in
the efficacy of passes, belief opens the chakras to the healing process.

The medium makes longitudinal or transversal passes with the
hands, depending on what type of healing is required, along the front
of the body, then along the back, as Irma in the person of Zé da Mata
did for me at the beginning of this chapter. If the medium incorporates
a Preto Velho or Caboclo, the healing may be done with smoke from a
pipe or cigar. Longitudinal movements calm the patient; transversal
movements excite. Since a sacred locale enormously helps direct positive healing energies, the most startling and successful healings usually occur during charity sessions at terreiros.

▲ ▲ ▲

I hope that the botanicals and their rituals described in this chapter
will be useful additions to your healing arsenal, no matter what your
spiritual orientation is.

NOTES

1. Pompílio Possera de Eufrázio, *Catecismo do Umbandista* (Rio de Janeiro: Editora Eco, 1974), 128

2. Ibid., 124.

3. *Seu* plus the first name of a man is a title of respect that also sometimes carries a fond or friendly connotation. The word is short for *senhor*, and here
   means "Mr. Tom."

4. Antonio Teixeira Alves Neto, *Curas, Mandingas e Feitiços de Preto-Velho*, 4th ed.
   (Rio de Janeiro, Editora Eco, n.d.), 66.

5. The term *abô* comes from the Yoruba word *agbà*, meaning "infusion of herbs."

6. *Amaci* is a combination of the Yoruba words *amá*, meaning "custom," "habit," and *si*, "to put inside."

7. Uri Geller (1946–) is an Israeli psychic who has become famous by developing his powers of concentration to the point where he can bend spoons and other metal objects without touching them.

AFTERWORD

SARAVÁ, BRAZILIAN MAGICK!

I first came in contact with Afro-Brazilian religions when I traveled to Brazil on a Fulbright fellowship to complete the research for my doctoral thesis on *Os Sertões (Rebellion in the Backlands)* by Euclides da Cunha. This work brought me in direct contact with the power of Messainism, a cult that still lives and breathes in the northeast. Although this and other folk religions were referred to in this and other literary works, the academic community glossed over the significance of these sects to Brazilian life as quaint beliefs of the uneducated that really were not very important.

Because of my "academic acquaintance" with these religions I was astounded when I arrived in Rio to see just how thoroughly these seemingly primitive and exotic sects permeated the hearts and minds of the people. As I gained a surface knowledge of these sects, I was struck by the rigid hierarchical structure and complexity of the rules and regulations of the rituals that seemed to mirror Brazilian government and society as it was during the dictatorship.

Continuing to study these faiths, I became attracted to them at a deeper level. Perhaps it was the music and dancing, I don't know. Every time I attended a ritual I came away imbued with a feeling of vitality and joy. I sensed that underneath the ceremonial veneer something profound was going on. I persisted beyond the unfamiliar and apparently exotic ritual procedures, objects, legends, and language, and grew to respect and appreciate what these traditions have to offer.

For me, one intriguing feature is the sophisticated symbolic nature of these religions, especially Candomblé. What is first revealed to the "pilgrim" who chooses this path toward spiritual enlightenment is an outer door that when opened, leads to rooms and other doors, which in turn, uncover even more chambers that lie within until the dedicated aspirant eventually reaches a central core. Although I do not presume to have done more than penetrate the outer layers of the symbolic language of these religions, I believe that the essence that lies at the core has important implications for anyone who seriously assays the path to spiritual development. Although I realize I still do not, and may never completely understand these sects, I can perceive numerous parallels between the Afro-Brazilian and the Western Magickal Mystery Traditions, which I have also written about and some of which have been alluded to in this book. (See "Other Books by the Author" in the front of this book.)

One conclusion I draw from these similarities is that anyone who believes in the importance of spirituality in human life will find rich ground to pursue by studying these traditions.

The other noteworthy feature of these religions for me is what the attitudes, values, practices, and the beliefs they encompass say about Brazilians. I always heard that these traditions were a way to keep the poor in their places or that worshipping gods and goddesses represented a means by which the downtrodden could find solace in their otherwise joyless, hopeless lives. After studying these sects, as far as I am concerned, nothing is further from the truth. Such a stance views this phenomenon from the outside in narrow, socio-political terms with little or no understanding of the deep, spiritual probing that takes place within. What these religions show me is that Brazilians, a diverse group of people from all classes and conditions, can unite successfully in a common bond of mutual respect to develop their common need for a spiritually satisfying life. In the process, they have managed to attain a goal that none of us should ever lose sight of: the celebration of life.

So I say, Saravá Brazilian Magick! Salve to the magick of all the nations!

A User-Friendly Guide to Portuguese Pronunciation

Brazilian Portuguese is a beautiful, but decidedly difficult language to pronounce. Although the grammar is 60 to 70 percent like Spanish, many different terms have come into the language from African, Amerindian, and other sources, including the inventive, prolific, and ever-changing slang. This makes the language very hard for even a native Spanish speaker to understand. An added complexity is presented by the rich variety of dialects that are spoken throughout the country.

In the guide that follows, the pronunciation is that of the Carioca dialect, that is, Portuguese as pronounced in Rio de Janeiro. This dialect was chosen for several reasons. Carioca Portuguese is what is spoken on the influential television network, TV Rede Globo, the fourth-largest television station in the world. The station reaches all corners of the country and serves to help unify the people. Carioca Portuguese is also the accent spoken in films and music, because Rio is still considered the "Paris" or cultural capital of the country. It represents the accent with which travelers and students of Brazil are most likely to come in contact. Last, but certainly not least, Carioca Portuguese is what I speak.

Brazilians pronounce their vowels in several ways, depending on whether the letter is stressed or unstressed; if it appears in a word that is masculine, feminine, singular, or plural; whether it crops up in a verb or a noun; or if the letter is followed by certain consonants. I do not describe dipthongs (vowel combinations) in this guide because I do not want to overwhelm you with the number of possible double and triple vowel combinations. Just try to combine the single vowel sounds.

The good news is that consonants are generally easier to get acquainted with because many of them sound as they do in English. However, some of them present their own peculiarities. For example, an "x" can be pronounced at least four different ways.

It is also noteworthy that Portuguese is a nasal language with few equivalents for these sounds in English. If you practice your pronunciation when you have a head cold you will be amazed at your progress!

All African terms pass through "Portuguesezation," that is, they are pronounced as if they were Brazilian Portuguese words. Also, Potuguese words are often (though not always) stressed on the next to the last syllable (as in **Sal** ve). If you see an accent mark somewhere else in the word, stress that syllable (Orixá).

With these details in mind, here is an attempt to present some English approximations for Portuguese sounds. I am sure that if you mispronounce anything the Orixás will understand!

Boa sorte! Good luck!

Single Vowels

a   When stressed, this vowel sounds like a person trying to appear posh when pronouncing the first "a" in "art noveau." When unstressed, it sounds like the combination of the "u" in "mug" and the "ai" in "certain."

al   This is the first of the infamous "back vowels," meaning that it is pronounced in the back of the throat, and you never actually enunciate the "l." The best approximations I can think of are a combination of the "al" in "paltry" and the "ow" in "cow," or the "au" in "assault."

ã, am, an   Followed by an "m," "n," or "nh," or with a squiggly mark called a til (~) over the vowel, these are signs of nasalization or closing down of the vowel.

e   This can be "close" or "open" when stressed, which means that it either sounds like the "ei" in "eight" or the "e" in "bet." When unstressed, this vowel is usually pronounced like the "ee" in "weenie" or if you prefer, the "oui" in "Ouija board."

el   A back vowel pronounced a little like the "el" in the Denver Broncos' famous quarterback's last name, "John Elway." Then again, it also sounds like the "ea" in meal."

ẽ, em, en   A nasalized sound, somewhat like the "ai" in "paint," only nasalized, of course.

i   The "i" is generally pronounced like an unstressed Portuguese "e," that is, like the "e" in "eat." It can also be pronounced like the "i" in "pencil" or "winter."

il   Another pesky back vowel that sounds a little like the English words "ill" and "eel."

ĩ, im, in   Another nasal vowel, remotely pronounced like the "ui" in "penguin."

o   As with the Portuguese "e," when this vowel is stressed, it is either "close" or "open." There are rules governing close and open vowels, but if you think this mini-guide is difficult to master, you should read these Byzantine grammatical rules. For your purposes, assume that the "o" when stressed is either like the "o" of "oat" or the "ou" in "ought." To master the open "o," repeat several times, "Oshkosh, by gosh!" When unstressed, the "o" has an "oo" sound like when you "croon 'doobie doobie doo.'"

ol   This is pronounced a bit like the "a" in "all."

õ, om, on If you were a goose you could nasalize a "honk" with perfect Portuguese enunciation of the nasalized "o."

u   This is an "oo" sound. Think "cootie catcher."

ul   This high back vowel definitely sounds like the "ul" and "oo" in "mulberry fool."

ũ, um, un The nasal "oo" sound occurs, as far as I know, in only one word: *muito*. Unfortunately, it is a common word that means "much," "a lot," and "very."

y   Pronounced as in English ("yes!") and occurs only in foreign words, like one spelling of the name of the goddess Yemanjá. The same sound in native Portuguese is spelled "ie."

CONSONANTS

b   This letter is pronounced as in English.

c   "Ca," "co," and "cu" are pronounced hard, like the "c" in "cop." "Ce" and "ci" are pronounced soft, like the "c" in "cellar."

d   "Da," "do," "du" and stressed "di," "de" are pronounced as in English, except that the tip of the tongue is against the teeth, not the gum ridge. "Detective Dodder did the deed." However, unstressed "de" and "di" usually are pronounced in Carioca Portuguese as "dgee," which is something like the "g" in "genie" or the "j" in "jeep."

f   Pronounced as in English.

g   "Ga," "go," and "gu" sound hard, like "gopher." "Ge" and "gi" are soft like the "z" in "azure."

h   This letter, for some obscure grammatical reason, is never pronounced. It is always silent. Ignore it.

j   This is a sexy consonant, pronounced soft, like the soft "g" or like the "zs" of "Zsa Zsa Gabor."

k   This is a hard "c" sound as in English "car," and is only used in foreign words.

l   Enunciated similarly to the English "l," only the tongue "lingers more lovingly on the letter."

m   This usually sounds like the "m" in "mother," but if preceded by a vowel and at the end of a syllable, it is silent, and indicates nasalization of the preceding vowel.

n   Like the "m," "n" is equivalent to the same sound in English, and it behaves nasally like an "m" at the end of a syllable when preceded by a vowel.

p   Approximates an English "p," only it is somewhat softer, though not as soft as in Spanish. Repeat several times: "I'll have pea soup, please."

q   A hard "k" sound like in "kilo."

r   If it occurs as the first letter of a word, before another consonant, at the end of a word, or doubled (rr), it has a gurgling sound, like the hard "h" of "halt" or the "ch" of "Bach." If it occurs singly between vowels, after a consonant, or at the end of a word where the previous letter is a vowel and the first letter of the next word starts with a vowel, it is pronounced like the "d" of "heeding." (This, for all you linguistics buffs, is called a "voiced dental flap.") If you can master the "r," nasalization, and back vowels, the rest of the language is a snap!

s   Like an English "s," as in "silly" at the beginning of a word, and like a "z" between vowels and before voiced consonants. (A voiced consonant occurs when your vocal cords vibrate, as when you say "d," "b," and "g.") At the end of a word or phrase, an "s" can sound like a "z" or a "sh" or "zjh." Don't worry, this is a fine point. It will not interfere with anyone understanding you.

t   "Ta," "to," and "tu" and stressed "te" and "ti" are pronounced like the "t" in the English word "toe," only the tip of the tongue lies against the teeth, not the gum ridge. "Te" and "ti" when unstressed are usually pronounced in Carioca Portuguese as a "tschee." Pretend you are going to sneeze, or say "Tallahatche Bridge" or "chief."

v   Said just like an English "v" as in "Viking."

w   Pronounced as in English, but only used in foreign words, usually names, like "Waldemir" and "Oswaldino." Portuguese often substitutes and pronounces a "v" for a "w."

x   This consonant can sound like the "sh" in "shell" (as in words like Oxum, Oxóssi, and Orixá), the "s" in "Sam," the "x" in "existential," or the "z" in "zebra."

z   "Zebra" will work, but sometimes it is pronounced like a Portuguese "j" as in "measure," or the "s" in "Sally."

ch   Say it like the "sh" in "sherry."

lh   Sounds like the "ll" in "million."

nh   Equivalent to the Spanish "ñ" sound. If you don't speak Spanish, try saying *nyet* in Russian. If that doesn't work for you, say "canyon" or "onion."

c, ss, sc   Pronounced like the "s" in "sea."

PERSONAS OF THE ORIXÁS

For quick reference, this appendix lists the characteristics of the Orixás. It includes the African meanings of their names and the Roman Catholic and other honorary names—all of which give clues to their characters. The elements they control, their dominions and the symbols they carry, their colors, the way they dress, their dance steps, colors of their guias, and how they are greeted in the terreiro will help you recognize them. Offertory foods for each Orixá can be found in Appendix D.

Like other aspects of the rituals, the Orixás' personal characteristics differ from sect to sect, so I have attempted to include only the traits that appear most frequently. I must admit that I hit a brick wall when it came to identifying the day of the week on which each entity is honored. Every sect, and even terreiros within the same sect, designate so many different days that I almost would need to list every day for each divinity.

Persona of Iansã

Names:	Iansã, Oyá (named for an African river), St. Barbara; Yoruba *ìya*, "mother;" *sán*, "thunder"—the thunder mother, goddess of the storm, goddess of vengeance.
Dominion:	Wind, tempests, vengeance, the Eguns.
Colors:	Coral, yellow, red, brown, white.
Stones/Metals:	Blue granite, meteorite, coral.
Symbols:	*Iruexim*, also spelled *eruxim* (a whip made from the hair of a horse's tail), cutlass, copper chalice, lightning and thunderbolts.
Dance:	One hand on the waist, the other trembling in the wind, or holding a goblet in the palm.
Salutation:	*Eparrei!*
Dress:	Red and green clothing, with brass and copper bracelets; or a red skirt, with a red or white sash tied in front, and a copper crown with beaded fringe: or coral clothing, combined with yellow necklaces, large bangle bracelets.
Guias:	Red and coral, yellow and coral, or green beads.

Persona of the Ibêji

Names: Saints Cosmus and Damian, the Twins, Dois-Dois (Two-Two), the Erês (this shows a confusion with the actual Erês, who are childlike vibrations that emanate from each Orixá). Yoruba *ibi*, "birth;" *èji*, "two." The Twins are not considered Orixás in all temples.

Dominion: Duality, fertility, survival of the soul in double form, pregnancy.

Colors: Green, rose, red.

Stones/Metals: None discovered — perhaps silver or metal.

Symbols: Double scepter with two little gourds tied to it, a silver palm leaf, toys.

Dance: Skipping like a child.

Salutation: *Iá-o!* or *O-ni beijada!* or *Bejé o ró!* or *Lá ô!*

Dress: Gold-lined cape in green, rose, or red, metal helmet.

Guias: Pink, red, green, blue beads.

Persona of Iemanjá

Names: Yemanjá; Our Lady of the Conception, of the Rosary, or of the Sea; Virgin Mary, Virgin of Lourdes. Yoruba *yè yè*, "mother;" *omon*, a diminutive referring to animals; *eja*, "fish"—mother of the fish.

Dominion: Water, middle depths of the sea, mothers, wives, families.

Colors: Light milky blue, light pink, pure white.

Stones/Metals: White seashells, gold.

Symbols: Silver cutlass; star; *abebê*—a round, silver fan with the etched figure of a mermaid; silver half moon; silver fish; mermaid; seashell; white china bowls.

Dance: Soft movements of the hands as if parting the waters.

Salutation: *Odóia!* (mother of the river), or *Odô-fé-iabá!* (beloved river lady), or *Ora yê yê ô!*

Dress: Fringed crown with beads, bracelets, two silver fish attached at the waist, amulet necklace, blue skirt, white blouse, pink sash, white cloth at the waist over the skirt, blue sash tied around the head under the crown with the ends hanging down the back.

Guias: Crystal, silver, transparent white, or blue beads; seashells.

Persona of Nanã

Names: Tobossi, Borokô, Anamburucu Nanã Burukê. Yoruba *na, nón,* "oneself;" *buru,* "mad;" *ikú,* "separation of oneself, death;" *bu,* "to take a piece of something;" *ru,* "to generate;" *kú,* "to die." She is so named when she is linked with death. She is also known as St. Anne and *Mãe-d'água,* "Mother of the Water."

Dominion: Mother of the Orixás, Guardian of the Portal of Death, the deep sea, ruins, and deep wells.

Colors: White, dark blue, purple.

Stones/Metals: Cowrie shells, river or sea stones.

Symbols: *Ibiri* (a little broom made with Coastal straw, cowrie shells, and ribbons), from the Yoruba *ibi,* "birth;" *ri,* "previously."

Salutation: *Salubá!*

Dance: Curved over a cane like an old woman, moving slowly and unsteadily; the Dance of the Plates.

Dress: Blue and white skirt and blouse, necklaces.

Guias: Dark blue and milky white, or lilac-colored beads.

Persona of Ogum

Names: Ogun, St. George, St. Anthony, God of War, God of Demands.

Dominion: War, vengeance, sculpture, pottery, mining, iron-work, defender of the law, agriculture, surgery. (In Brazil, he is mostly seen as the god of war.)

Colors: Dark blue, red, white.

Stones/Metals: Magnetic stones, iron.

Symbols: Crossed swords; scalpel; sickle; breadfruit tree; seven, fourteen, or twenty-one instruments of war and agriculture affixed to an iron bow.

Dance: Stabbing the air with a sword.

Salutation: *Ogum Nhê!*

Dress: Dark blue pants and skirt, two dark blue beaded sashes, breastplate, helmet (sometimes plumed), bracelets and wrist bands, white metal sword.

Guias: Red and milky white; clear dark blue; green and blood red beads.

Persona of Omulu

Names: Omolu, Xampanã, Doctor of the Poor, Obaluaiê (younger), St. Bento, St. Rock, St. Lazarus. Yoruba *omu,* "sharp;" *oolu,* "hole-maker" (as in smallpox).

Dominion: Illness, smallpox, infectious diseases, cemeteries, sickbeds.

Colors: Scarlet, yellow, black, gray.

Stones/Metals: Cowrie shells.

Symbols: A miniature iron lance, two thick wooden clubs, three silver arrows, a bowl filled with cowrie shells, *xaxará de piassava* (a stick made of braided straw with cowrie shells, or of black or red thongs punched from leather; it represents epidemics that, like a broom, sweep the world of living beings).

Dance: Curved over a cane like an old man.

Salutation: *Atotô!* ("silence, listen").

Dress: *Filá*—a hood-like garment made of coastal straw decorated with cowrie shells. It covers the entire body, including the head. The garment is worn over a black-and-white skirt or a combination of black, white, yellow, and blue.

Guias: Alternate milky white and black, or black and milky yellow beads; a *laguidibá*, which is a necklace made from small coconut shells or sliced black bull horn pieces and black beads.

Persona of Oxalá

Names: Obatalá, Jesus Christ, Christ of the Bonfim, Father of the Orixás, Orixalá, Oxalufã (elder), Oxaguiã (younger). Yoruba *orixalá*, "the great Orixá."

Dominion: Procreation, creative force of nature, death, peace.

Colors: White, marble, gold.

Stones/Metals: Lead, silver, marble.

Symbols: Shepherd's staff; shells; white or lemon-lime colored circle; gold, lead, or silver ring; a pestle (to grind yams), cowrie shells.

Dance: When incorporated as a woman, she dances with an abebê called an *oxágiriã*.

Salutation: *Epá-Baba!* for Oxalufã; *Exê-ê-Babá!* for Oxaguiã.

Dress: White skirt with white lace blouse, silver bracelets.

Guias: Milky white beads, because this color is believed to synthesize them all.

Persona of Oxóssi

Names: Oxósse, Odê, St. Sebastian, St. George, St. Expedite, God of the Caboclos, God of the Forest and of the Hunt.

Dominion: The hunt, the forest, cultivation, the law of Christ.

Colors: Green and yellow, or green and white, light blue.

Stones/Metals: Stones from the jungle floor or forest brooks.

Symbols: Metal or painted wooden bow and arrow called an *ofá*; miniature rifle; fig tree; leather hat or crown with feathers; *capanga* (leather satchel) to hold game; acacia tree.

Dance: Gesture of shooting a bow and arrow, imitating hunting.

Salutation: *Okê!* or *Okê Arô!* or *Odê-Kakê-maiô!*

Dress: Printed green skirt, or green and blue skirt over white lace pants, a sash tied in the back, two sashes tied around the shoulders, silver helmet with blue and white plumes, two bracelets and two metal wrist bands, breastplate.

Guias: Green and white, green and yellow, or light blue and cherry red beads.

Persona of Oxum

Names: Oxun; Our Lady of the Rosary, Conception, Carmo, and Candeia; St. Catherine. She is named for an African river.

Dominion: Femininity, charity, the womb, the middle depths of the sea.

Colors: Gold, yellow, blue.

Stones/Metals: Yellow brass, river rocks, shells found in running water.

Symbols: Abebê, dagger, tumbled river stones, ofá (because she is Oxóssi's wife), pot of water, white china bowls, bells, mirrors, makeup, toilet water, dove.

Dance: Like a woman taking a bath in the river, sensually combing her hair.

Salutation: *Eri ieiê ô!* or *Ora ieiê ô!*

Dress: Fringed *adê*, which is a beaded metal or silk crown; bracelets, rings, wrist bands; fine lace blouse in yellow cloth of a color lighter than the skirt; long, golden yellow skirt; sash tied over the breasts and falling over the back; necklace with charms of little combs, mirrors, fish, spoon—all made out of brass.

Guias: Yellow, gold, light blue, or milky blue beads.

Persona of Oxumarê

Names: St. Bartholomew (sometimes, but this Orixá really has no Roman Catholic counterpart), Berrém or St. Barbara (when a female). Yoruba *osumàarè,* "rainbow."

Dominion: The rainbow, the sky.

Colors: White, green.

Stones/Metals: Aerolite.

Symbols: Two iron cobras clasped in the hand, iron trident, broom, sword, dove.

Dance: Like a snake.

Salutation: *Arô Boboi!* or *Arô Moboi!*

Dress: Sometimes green- and yellow-dyed cowries on his clothes; skirt and top all in white with a green sash; crown of braided ribbons all the colors of the rainbow including blue, yellow, pink, green, and white; cowrie bracelet; two sashes worn crosswise, one over one shoulder, and the other under the other shoulder made from cowries.

Guias: Cowrie shells, shiny or milky green beads, or alternating yellow and green beads.

Persona of Xangô

Names: St. Gerome, St. Michael Archangel, St. Peter, St. John, God of Lightning and Justice. Various names are added to his first name to show his multifaceted character. The word *Xangô* also refers to a kind of Gegê-Nagô ritual practiced in the northeastern states of Pernambuco, Alagoas, Sergipe, and Paraíba.

Dominion: Law, justice, tempests, knowledge, institution of the law.

Colors: Red, brown, white, purple.

Stones/Metals: Meteorite, black stones collected from waterfalls.

Symbols: Double-bladed ax (*oxê*), thunder and lightning bolts, javelin, *xaque-xaque* (a type of percussion instrument).

Dance: Clenched fists boxing each other; a sword fight is bound to ensue whenever Ogum descends in the same terreiro at the same time (because the two warriors harbor a longstanding disagreement over Iansã).

Salutation: *Kauô Kabiecile!* or *Caô Cabecilha!*

Dress: Short skirt with red and white panels; red sash tied in back, and two white sashes crossed under the red one ending in knots falling in front; copper bracelets; a king's crown.

Guias: Deep red and white, or light brown (for justice).

SOME TROPICAL BOTANICALS USED IN BRAZILIAN MAGICK

The botanicals and their uses listed here are given as matters of curiosity and are not intended as substitutes for medical care. Many of the botanicals are dangerously poisonous.

Acácia or Jurema

Names: Acacia, gum arabic (*A. senegal*), koa wood (Hawaii), mimosa, wattle bark (Australia), *Acacia* genus; jurema branca (*Pithecolobium diversifolium*). There are more than 800 subspecies of this botanical.

Associations: Oxóssi.

Medicine:	The leaf is applied externally in baths or compresses to cure ulcers or cankers. Internally, a decoction can be taken to relieve the symptoms of coughs, diarrhea, and typhus. Do not burn the leaf.
Uses:	Purification baths, bead and washes, amacis.

In the Catimbó cults, the Indians prepare a drink extracted from the root, which they call *Cauim* or *Ajucá*. After drinking the decoction, they claim they feel so lightweight that they are transported to the sky.

In Belém, the capital of the northern state of Pará, this tree is associated with Jureminha, a sister of the Cabocla spirit Jurema, who is thought to inhabit this tree and work on the White Line of magick. Many Indians of this region believe in her powers to grant their wishes and cure their ills, so it is not unusual to come across a jurema tree surrounded by offerings, including honey, candles, and perfume.

Acacia wood is also used in Western Witchcraft and Ceremonial Magick, but it is not ingested. The branches provide wands for general magick, and the resin of gum arabic when burned is said to attract friendly spirits and open the psychic centers; so there is a link between how it is used by Witches and Magicians and practitioners of Catimbó.

Alamanda

Names:	Common allamanda (*Alamanda cathartica*).
Associations:	Omulu, Oxum.
Medicine:	A useful plant for skin diseases, measles, eczema, furunculosis. Make a lotion from a decoction of the leaves, rind, or sap. Take a bath in the leaves to relieve scabies and lice.
Uses:	Amacis, purification baths. This climbing ornamental has whorled leaves and deep yellow or violet-colored flowers.

Alecrim

Names: Rosemary, incensier (*Rosmarinus officinalis*). Alecrim do Mato (*Baccharis silvestris*) is a related plant; it is a kind of thistle that is sometimes substituted. The only difference between this species and the garden variety is that it grows two to three feet high. Rosemary is a tender shrubby perennial that thrives in coastal areas; in fact, in the days of schooners, sailors could sense that land was nearby when they caught a whiff of its cleanly fragrant perfume.

Associations: Oxalá, Oxóssi.

Medicine: Imbibed as a tea, it is an excitant and effective remedy for coughs, indigestion, typhoid fever, intestinal gas, and lack of appetite. In a lotion, it can be taken to erase scarified wounds and to lessen the pain of articular rheumatism.

Uses: Amulets, ritual baths to drive away Exu and the Eguns, amacis, bead washes, personal and environmental incenses. It is one of the most popular ingredients in many purification incenses.

This is another botanical that crosses over between African and European traditions. Because people in Great Britain and Northern Europe for a long time did not have access to the fragrant gums such as frankincense and myrrh of the southern climes, they burned fragrant herbs such as rosemary, thyme, and lavender that grew easily in the region. This is the reason so many Celtic/Druidic incense recipes include this herb. In Western folk symbology, rosemary stands for fidelity in love, and of course, for remembrance. It is a key ingredient of Witches' Holy Water. Perhaps the sweet and clean odor of the burning leaves has led it to be revered and associated with many of the same symbols in both traditions.

Alface

Names: Lettuce (*Lactuca sativa*).

Associations: The Eguns, Iansã (because she is said to have conquered death).

Medicine: In folk medicine, lettuce is drunk in syrup form as a calmative for insomnia.

Uses: An important element of secret Egun ceremonies and Vumbi rites. The tea, concocted from the leaf, is recommended for chasing away disturbances caused by the Eguns.

The Greek legend tells that when the gods became enraged with Adonis, his mother Aphrodite hid him in a field of lettuce, covering him with the broad leaves. In this way he remained for many long years protected from the wrath of the other gods.

In Umbanda, an offering is made to the Eguns by placing a head of lettuce exactly in the center of a white china plate. Leaves from another head are distributed around the plate, and olives and vinegar are added to make a kind of salad. Then the petitioner places a piece of paper with a petition written on it in the center of the head, and carefully closes the leaves over it so that the wish remains hidden from the Eguns and they will not interfere with its being granted.

It is interesting to note that in European Witchcraft, wild lettuce (not exactly the same plant, but close) was one of the ingredients of the Witches' Flying Ointment with which Witches allegedly rubbed their bodies before flying off to Sabbats on their broomsticks.

Alfavaca
var. Alfavaca Roxa, Manjericão

Names: Basil, var. purple basil (*Ocimum basilicum*).

Associations: Obaluaiê, Oxalá, Oxóssi, Iansã, Oxum, Xangô, Iroko.

Medicine: Improves the digestion and helps eliminate intestinal gas. A decoction of the leaves provides a syrup for whooping cough. The leaves are also diuretic and diaphoretic. This culinary herb is also ingested in cases of nervous debility, pains in the kidneys, and burning urination.

Uses: Amacis, bead washes, purification baths, abô baths for the mediums of the appropriate Orixás.

Prepare a decoction of the leaves to feed Oxóssi's stones at his altar weekly. Basil is considered an effective amulet against lightning, thunderbolts, and storms, especially if it is burned in an incense. The incense also rids the area of obsessed spirits. This botanical holds tremendous power for the children of Xangô.

In Western Witchcraft, this herb enjoys a somewhat different reputation as an aphrodisiac, and promoter of fertility and prosperity. It is alleged to deter thieves and vandals.

Alfazema

Names: Lavender (*Lavandula genus*).

Associations: All the Orixás.

Medicine: Drink the tea to help cure persistent coughs, asthma, amennorhea, birthing problems, and kidney, liver, and spleen disorders.

Uses: Abô baths, amacis, bead washes, personal and environmental incenses. The spikes and branches also comprise ritual perfumes and sachets.

Along with rosemary, lavender is one of the most ubiquitous botanicals used in Afro-Brazilian ritual preparations. In Western Witchcraft, this herb is added to charm bags to bring peace, balance, and prosperity to the home. In Voodoo, which also has much in common with the Afro-Brazilian traditions, lavender comprises one of the principal ingredients of Four Thieves Vinegar, which is used for various magickal purposes.

Alões, Erva Babosa, or Azevre

Names: Aloe vera (*Aloe succotrina*).

Associations: Exu, Omulu, Ogum.

Medicine: The milky substance contained on the inside of the lanceolate leaf can be applied to burns, hemorrhoids, abscesses, and tumors as an emollient and blood coagulant. As this plant is difficult to dry, the Century Plant is often substituted. As a plant sacred to Ossãe, Orixá of botanicals, it is considered a fitting replacement for any herb.

Uses: Abô baths, bead washes, personal incenses for the mediums of Omulu.

Little correspondence seems to exist between the magickal uses of this succulent perennial of the lily family in Afro-Brazilian traditions and Western Witchcraft. In the latter tradition, aloe is considered a Venusian botanical, capable of drawing love, and an emblem of religious faith. In ancient Egypt, pilgrims who made journeys to faraway lands for religious purposes hung it from their doorways as proof of their piety.

Amendoeira

Names: Almond tree (*Prunus amygdalus communis*).

Associations: Exu, the Eguns.

Medicine: Odorless sweet almond oil, which is a fine emollient and provides the base for many massage oils. Bitter almond oil, which is the familiar signature scent of Jergens' lotion, is valuable in perfumery.

Uses: Purification baths. The pressed oil from the nuts is used to water Exu's *otá*. The oil is believed to store negative fluids during the day, and release them into the terreiro yard overnight.

Not much exists in common between the uses of this tree in Afro-Brazilian Magick and Western Occultism. In Witchcraft, because of its association with a Greek legend, the tree is considered a symbol of undying love and affection. A drop of bitter almond oil added to prosperity oil is said to bring quick results. The wood provides wands for general magick.

Araçá Do Campo

Names: Guava, strawberry guava (*Psidium littorale, P. guineense*).

Association: Oxóssi.

Medicine: The fruit is effective against diarrhea and urinary tract infections.

Uses: The leaves of this small tropical fruit tree are used in amacis, bead washes, environmental incenses, decorations for the terreiro for Caboclo festivals of the Angolan tradition. Children of Oxóssi beautifully decorate trays with guava leaves and fill them with food for his feast days.

Araticum-de-Aréia
or Biribá or Malôlo

Names: Custard apple, soursop (*Annona* genus).

Associations: Obaluaiê, Oxum, Iemanjá.

Medicine: The fruit pulp helps drain tumors, and the decoction of the leaves treats rheumatism. It is also an ingredient of sherbet and makes a refreshing drink.

Uses: This small tree that bears heart-shaped fruit is well known to the Bantu people, principally in the Congo and Angola. Its ritual attributes have translated to Brazil, where it is employed principally as a strong purification bath when a person is enmeshed in desperate circumstances. Many species of this family thrive in Brazil, all of which are used for the same ritual purposes.

Aroeira

Names: California pepper tree (*Schinus molle*). This tall tree is planted along avenues and on lawns.

Associations: Exu, Ogum.

Medicine: An anti-rheumatic, anti-syphilitic, and febrifuge. The leaves are used to treat skin ulcerations.

Uses: Amacis, initiation baths, heavy-duty purification baths.

To perform a strong purification bath, grind the pepper with purple pine needles, tilia tree leaves, broomweed, and ash leaves. Form a triangle by placing three lighted white candles around the patient. Begin the ritual at midnight in the middle of the triangle. Purify the patient with a mixture of flour, honey, and cachaça. Rub the affected person's body with the wings of a live chicken and dove, then follow with the purification bath. At the conclusion of the ritual, tear the person's clothes into rags, and dress her/him in clean white clothing.

To rid a person of Exu's influence, follow the same procedure, but afterwards, have the patient sit on a woven straw mat for a few hours.

One would think that since this tree is also native to California, and since it also grows large clusters of decorative, currant-like fruit that it would have a use in Western magickal traditions, but as far as I have been able to discover, it does not.

Arrebenta-Cavalos

Names: Harebell (*Isotoma longiflora*), soda apple night-shade (*Solanum aculeatis simum*). The name in Portuguese means "horsebreaker."

Associations: Obaluaiê, Exu.

Uses: Like California pepper, it is used in strong purification baths from the neck down, preferably at midnight with the patient in the center of a crossroads.

Note: Some 1,000 subspecies of herbs, shrubs, climbers, and trees belong to this group, but this plant does not exhibit thorns, and the leaves are dentate, soft, and milky-looking. Not recommended for medicinal use as it is extremely poisonous.

Arruda

Names: Rue, herb-of-grace (*Ruta graveolens*).

Associations: All the Orixás.

Medicine: Vermifuge, calmative, strong emmenagogue, anti-rheumatoid. The juice helps close wounds.

Uses: The properties of rue in Afro-Brazilian magick resemble those attributed to the botanical in Western Witchcraft. The herb foils the evil eye, cuts envy, counteracts black magick, and confers the blessings of the Orixás. Rue is worn around the neck in a sachet bag with other protective herbs as an amulet against evil.

Bambu

Names: Bamboo (*Bambusa arundinacea*).

Associations: The Eguns, Iansã.

Medicine: No medicinal uses found.

Uses: Decorate the house of the Eguns with this botanical. The leaves pulverized in incense and combined with sugar cane drive away obsessed spirits. Certain Caboclos are said to live in bamboo trees.

Bananeira

Names: Banana tree (*Musa genus*, especially *M. Paradisiaca*).

Associations: All the Orixás.

Medicine: Bananas are high in potassium, and help supplement diets poor in this mineral. *Banana do Brejo* is used as a gargle and the tiny forest banana is a good antidiuretic.

Uses: This twenty-foot tall tree of mystery and enchantment with its narrow, creamy, sweet yellow fruit does not belong to any particular Orixá, but rather to all of them. The tree is so revered that the leaves are used by the ecologically minded practitioners in rituals as a substitute for platters and other dishes where sacred food and botanicals are offered. Many different kinds of bananas are native to Brazil, and they are all used in magick.

Barba-de-Velho

Names:	Fennel flower (*Nigella arvensis*).
Associations:	Obaluaiê, Oxalá.
Medicine:	Apply a decoction of the juice topically to combat hemorrhoids.
Uses:	Amacis, abô baths, bead washes, incenses burned after purification baths.

Beldroega

Names:	Purslane (*Portulaca oleracea*).
Associations:	Obaluaiê, Exu, Irokô.
Medicine:	Apply the pulverized leaves topically to wounds that have built up scar tissue. The effect is rapid due to salycilic acid, the active principle of the plant. This botanical is also a galactogogue and diuretic, and the juice cures eye inflammations.
Uses:	This small plant with little obovate flowers and fleshy, succulent leaves is alleged to rid a person of nightmares provoked by negative astral influences.

This is also an important botanical in the purification of Exu's otás. First, clean the stone that is going to have its power fixed with Coastal soap (a kind of hard-milled Castille soap), then rub the stone with purslane and other botanicals meant for this purpose as described elsewhere in this herbal. Carry the otá to Exu's altar.

Brincos-de-Princesa

Names: Fuchsia (*Fuchsia integrifolia*). The name of this shrub with funnel-shaped flowers means "princess' earrings" in Portuguese.

Associations: Elegbara, Oxóssi.

Uses: Purification baths at crossroads during "open" hours (midnight, dawn, dusk). Use only after the necessary purification rites have been performed.

Cana

Names: Sugar cane (*Saccharum officinarum*).

Associations: Exu.

Uses: Cane is prepared in a special way and offered up to the entity on his altar. First, the raw cane must be husked, and peeled pieces are cut into sections down the center. The leaves and husks are burned in purification incenses. Sugar extracted from the cane is burned in incenses to destroy astral larvae and drive away the Eguns. The botanical is alleged to attract good fortune.

Sugar cane merits a special stature in Brazilian agriculture because it was the first crop successfully harvested in the country on a large scale, and rendered the first real wealth for the Portuguese colony. Cultivation was concentrated in the northeast region where gracious plantations, like those built on the cotton trade in the South of the U.S., flourished throughout the Colonial era. Also, as was the case with cotton, sugar cane production was labor-intensive. Because of the small native population, the Colonists imported slaves from Africa to perform the work. Sugar cane necessarily became an important part of Afro-Brazilian life, and consequently, has entered into folk religious rites.

Capeba, Pariparoba, or Cipó-de-Cobra

Names: A tropical herb of the pepper family with aromatic medicinal roots and oil-bearing, anise-scented fruit (*Pothomorphe peltata* or *Cissampelos glaberrima*). The pareira vine of the moonseed family is sometimes substituted.

Associations: The downy leaves of this tropical vine are sacred to Oxum and the entire plant belongs to Xangô and Oxóssi.

Medicine: A tea made from the leaves treats the liver, and a decoction of the roots makes an effective diuretic for uterine problems.

Uses: Abô baths, ori amacis, bead washes.

Capim-Limõ

Names: Lemongrass (*cymbopogon citratus*).

Associations: Oxalá, Oxóssi; in the northeast it is known as "incense of the Caboclo."

Medicine: Good for stomach troubles, colds, coughs.

Uses: Abô baths, head washes, amacis. Burn it as an incense to attract Caboclos and Boiadeiros (spirits of cowboys).

Cebola do Mato or Cencém

Names: Forest onion (*Amaryllis belladona* or *Hyacinthina grifinia*). They are mutually substitutable in magick.

Associations: Obaluaiê, Exu.

Medicine: Grate the onion and apply it topically to skin tumors. A decoction of the leaves pressed to a wound will help close it. A decoction can relieve asthma and other pulmonary congestion, but it can be toxic.

Uses: Cut into quarters and secrete in the corners of a room or under furniture to drive away liars, envious enemies, hypocrites, et cetera.

Coco de Iri

Names: The fruit of a type of coconut (*Astrocaryum ayri*).

Associations: Oxóssi, Iemanjá.

Medicine: A decoction of the root alleviates pain caused by female troubles when added to a bath or douche.

Uses: A discharge bath is made from the tree's fronds.

Coco de Dendê

Names: Dendê coconut (*Elaeis guineensis*).

Associations: Ossãe, Ifá, Exu.

Medicine: The powdered resin and leaves treat headaches, angina, diminished vision, leg swelling, and colic of the abdomen.

Uses: This palm, which grows from forty-five to ninety feet high, is one of the best known of Brazilian trees. Dendê palm oil is either orange or whitish to clear in color. It is a reasonable substitute for butter, making an indispensable ingredient in Afro-Brazilian cooking (see Appendix D), and imparting a distinctive flavor to these dishes. It is high in vitamins—important in a country where the average person cannot afford to eat a healthy diet—and it

provides a key ingredient for ritual dishes offered
to the Orixás.

Espada de São Jorge or Espada de Ogum

Names: "St. George's sword" (*Sansieveria ceylanica*). One
of the names for this plant in Portuguese means
"mother-in-law's tongue" because it has long, hard,
fibrous leaves that end in a sharp point.

Associations: Ogum.

Uses: Amacis and incenses for the children of Ogum. This
botanical is attributed with great protective powers
said to counteract black magick.

Estoraque Brasileiro

Names: Brazilian storax (*Styrax officinalis*).

Associations: Obaluaiê, Oxalá.

Medicine: Powder the resin and leaves to treat varicose ulcers.

Uses: Use the resin of this orange-flowered, benzoin-like
shrub in amacis and purification baths. Mixed
with benzoin and lavender, it makes an ideal
incense to use after personal discharge baths.

Fedegoso or Cádia

Names: Seaside heliotrope, shower of gold, pudding pine
(*Cassia fistula*). The Latin name refers to a genus of
plants of the *Leguminosae* family. This particular
plant grows on cylindrical stalks with wrinkled
leaves and lily or violet-colored tubular flowers.

Associations: Exu, Ogum.

Medicine: The nut, which is found inside a chocolate-colored bean, is a very strong emmenagogue that will cause miscarriage in pregnant women. The roasted roots are considered a tonic. Use the plant in homeopathic doses only to help alleviate the pains of pleurisy and to assuage fear.

Uses: Environmental purification incense and ritual baths. Usually it accompanies other botanicals that are used for identical purposes. An infusion of the herb is employed as a floorwash where Exu's sigil has been previously scratched on the floor with chalk. Seaside heliotrope is also offered to Ogum, the god of war, before undertaking any battle or altercation.

Figo

Names: Common fig tree (*Ficus; F. carica*). Other names in Portuguese for the various figs are *Avelós, Figueira-do-diabo* (*Datura stramonium*), and *Gaiolinha. Figueira do Inferno* (literally "hell's fig") is the Barbados nut (*Jatropha curcas*).

Associations: Fig trees are held in high regard by practitioners of Brazilian Magick. See "Uses," below.

Medicine: A tea of the leaves is taken to alleviate the symptoms of intestinal and stomach problems and as an aid for digestion. Devil's fig counteracts vomiting and swelling of the testicles.

Uses: The gameleira, or white fig, sacred to Xangô and Nanã, is quite rare, and is the most prized tree of all. However, it is not often used anymore because it is practically extinct.

The balsam fig is a beautiful tree that produces large, dark brown-colored fruit in great quantities along its trunk. This tree was brought from Africa by a missionary, and planted in the northeast state of Pernambuco in 1892, so it is a relatively recent import. Be careful of the milk sap that runs down the trunk, because it can blind. The perfume exuded by the tree calls the attention of anyone who passes by. The dried leaves retain their wonderful scent for many years. The area around the trunk is deemed a place of concentration for Exu's energy; consequently, many offerings are left to him at the foot of the tree.

The Benjamin fig provides one of Exu's fetishes, and is also an ingredient in baths to put an end to persecutions or possessions by Exu. The root of this fruit tree, which grows primarily along the Rio State coast, is used by itself as an amulet against the evil eye. In Umbanda, the leaves are woven into crowns to celebrate a new Iaô's initiation.

For someone who is ascertained to be suffering persecution from Exu, a purification bath is made from a decoction of the leaves. Then the patient is positioned in the middle of a seesaw and bathed. When the bath is finished, the seesaw is tipped so the water can run off the patient's back, taking with it all of Exu's negativity.

Folha-da-Fortuna or Folha-de-Oxalá

Names: Life plant, air plant (*Kalanchoé brasiliensis*). The name in Portuguese means "fortune herb" or "Oxalá's herb." This is because the leaves are able to engender new plants, and the greater or lesser number of plants that develop are said to foretell one's fortune.

Associations: Oxalá, Exu.

Uses: Purification baths and an appropriate abô for a
child of almost any Orixá. The liquid, which is
obtained by maceration of the leaves, is sprinkled
over the floor of the area where the future initiate is
sequestered. This botanical is said to confer good
luck on anyone who keeps it in the home. The bush
grows about three feet high and produces lovely,
orange-yellow flowers.

Guiné-de-Caboclo, Erva-de-Guiné, or Ervapipí

Names: Guinea grass (*Petiveria tetranda*).

Associations: Iansã, Exu, the Eguns.

Uses: A plant with many magickal uses. The roots of the
grass are made into amulets to protect a person
from obsessed spirits and to cleanse people and
places. Crowns fashioned from the grass are conferred on mediums during initiation ceremonies.

Hissopo or Alfazema de Caboclo

Names: Hyssop, holy herb (*Hyssopus officinalis*).

Associations: Because of its many virtues hyssop is considered
sacred to all of the Orixás.

Medicine: As part of the Brazilian folk medicine chest this
botanical is valuable for respiratory ailments,
and is added as an expectorant in anticatarrhal
syrups.

Uses: Spiritual cleansing, amacis, bead washes, baths.

Hyssop is another herb that crosses over to various magickal traditions. In Witchcraft it is also a symbol of purification and is alleged to
help open the psychic centers.

Hortelã-Pimenta

Names:	Peppermint (*Mentha piperita*).
Associations:	Oxalá, Exu.
Medicine:	A tea brewed from the leaves quells flatulence, indigestion, nervous vomiting, and intestinal cramps, and helps expel worms. It is also a galactogogue and good headache remedy.
Uses:	Peppermint is a decoration for Exu's altar. It is also an ingredient of discharge baths from the neck down, because it is alleged to cancel out negative fluids. Peppermint also charges the liquid for otá purifications.

An interesting parallel occurs with the ritual use of peppermint in Brazilian Magick and Western Occultism where the essence of the herb in both systems is considered an activator of spells. One drop added, let's say, to a love perfume, attracts a lover posthaste!

Jaborandí

Name:	*Pilocarpus jaborandixaps.*
Associations:	Ogum.
Medicine:	The leaves of this bush make a superb wash for oily hair, and are also applied in tonics to help make hair grow. The oil from the glands in the leaves are also used to fight glaucoma. Jaborandí also brings on sweats in cases of pleurisy, bronchitis, and fevers, and helps stop pulmonary edema and hemorrhage.
Uses:	Amacis, abôs, bead washes, baths. It is also used to "take away the hand from the head," that is, remove the influence of a priest or priestess from an initiate in a ceremony called Removal of the

Hand of Vumbi. A ceremony like this happens, for example, when a Babalorixá or Ialorixá dies.

Jenipapapeiro

Names: Genipap, genip, marmalade box (*Genipapa americana*). The name refers to about six subspecies of trees of the *Rubiaceae* family. The tree can grow to a height of fifty feet, and has obovate to oblong leaves and long white or pale yellow, silky flowers. The wood is strong and flexible, so is used for carriage wheels, rims, spokes, boat ribs, tennis racquets, barrel hoops, and tool handles. The orange-sized fruit is edible, but not palatable. A blue dye is extracted to paint the bodies of practitioners in Amerindian rituals.

Associations: Ossãe, Iroko, Obaluaiô.

Medicine: Boil the leaves together with bark chips to extract a juice to work on varicose ulcers.

Uses: The fruit renders an indelible blue dye that is used for body paint in Catimbó rituals. The country folk of northern Brazil distill a wine from the juice. The leaves are an ingredient of purification baths.

It is widely believed that genipap can eliminate epilepsy attacks and halt the ravages of time, despite the fact that such conditions are considered incurable. The patient is stood against a tree. To one side, three candles are placed in the form of a triangle, then lighted. The practitioner takes a brand-new, steel-bladed knife in hand and kneels beside the tree praying to Ossãe and Irokô to eradicate the evil. Then she/he rises and cuts the tree with the knife, at the same time saying, "As I cut this tree so shall the evil be cut from this ailing person."

Lágrima-de-Nossa-Senhora

Names: Job's tears (*Coix lacryma-jobi*). In Portuguese, this variety of grass with hard, droplike, grayish white seeds means "Tears of Our Lady."

Associations: Ossãe, Iemanjá.

Medicine: The tea is a diuretic and is also used in the bath to reduce rheumatic swellings. It is an excitant.

Uses: Many kinds of head obligations, abô baths, and purification baths. Do not boil this botanical. The water filtered from macerating the leaves and seeds makes an eye bath to help develop clairvoyance. Apply in the morning after leaving the water outside in a bowl during the night. Be sure to bring the bowl indoors before dawn.

Louro

Names: Bay laurel, sweet bay (*Laurus nobilis*).

Associations: Oxalá, Iansã.

Medicine: The leaves are a condiment. They are also useful medicinally for indigestion, anuria, bladder infections, and menstrual cramps.

Uses: As in Western Occultism, the leaves are renowned in divination and as a botanical that attracts good fortune and drives away negativity. Place the leaves as decorations around Iansã's sacred dish, *acarajé*, when praying for her to be merciful.

Malva do Campo or Malvarisco

Names: Any of various small, resinous shrubs (*Kielmeyera* genus), all native to Brazil; also a botanical of the Malvaceae family, possibly musk mallow with flowers resembling mallows or camellias.

Associations: Oxalá, Oxóssi, Nanã, Exu.

Medicine: Helps cure abscesses, gingivitis, sore throat, and inflammations arising from mouth operations. The roots, leaves, and flowers are all used.

Uses: Purification and abô baths, particularly for the children of Nanã; an otá cleanser; a decoration for Exu's altar. Malva is held in high repute as a botanical for mediumistic development and is used in some secret Candomblé rites.

Mamona or Carrapateira

Names: Castor bean, Palma Christi (*Ricinus comunis*).

Associations: Exu.

Medicine: The rind is a purgative, but the seeds must be cleaned from it first, as they are highly toxic.

Uses: The pod serves as a receptacle for Exu's sacred dishes. It also fixes this entity's fetishes. A castor bean offering can also be made in order to perform a rite for personal discharge of negative energy. First, fill seven servings of the ebô into seven bean shells along with dendê oil. Each of the seven leaves represents one part of Exu's axé, or power, which is manifested by sacrificing a bird to him and spilling some of its blood on each ebô. Tie together the seven ebós and wrap them in a large piece of paper or cardboard. Then travel to seven crossroads, and at each one, leave one of the prepared shells as an offering to Exu along with a coin. In that way you are cured of the infestation.

Mangue Vermelho
or Mangue-Sapateiro

Names:　Mangle, American red mangrove (*Rhisophora mangle*).

Associations:　Obaluaiê, Omulu.

Medicine:　A decoction of the tannin-rich bark of this palm-like bush found along the seacoast and especially in the Amazon estuary alleviates varicose ulcers. Make a compress of the decoction of the small flowers to treat skin lesions.

Uses:　Initiation rites.

Mangueira

Names:　Mango tree (*Mangifera indica*).

Associations:　Exu, Ogum.

Medicine:　A syrup made from the pulp soothes bronchitis. The juice extracted from the branches is used against gonorrhea and diarrhea.

Uses:　The leaves are used in initiation rites. A purification bath from the neck down is prepared from a mixture of mango leaves, California pepper leaves, purple pine, cashew, and broomweed. In many Candomblé terreiros the leaves are spread on the floor to drive away evil fluids and astral larvae.

Melã-de-São-Caetano
or Erva-de-Cobra

Names:　Balsam apple, balsam pear (*Mamordica balsamina, M. charantia*). This plant of the gourd family bears small, yellowish red, gherkin-shaped fruit.

Association:　Xangô.

Medicine: The leaves are an anti-rheumatic and febrifuge that help lessen the discomfort of female illnesses. A pulp made from the seeds makes a fine unguent for inflammations.

Uses: Removes obsessed spirits; an ingredient of otá baths.

Noz de Cola or Obi

Names: Sudan cola (*Cola acuminata*). The nut of this sturdy evergreen native Brazilian tree originally went into making Coca-Cola. The seeds smell like roses.

Associations: Oxalá, Obatalá, and the other creator gods.

Medicine: Africans eat the fruit to refresh their energy. Cola nut is a heart tonic because it regulates the pulse. It also revives the nervous system, and is effective against anemia.

Uses: It is an especially indispensable ingredient in baths for the children of Oxalá when they are being sequestered during initiation rites. The only Orixá who does not accept a cola nut offering is Xangô. Cola nuts enter into almost all obligation ceremonies of the Afro-Brazilian cults. The nut is also used in divination to answer yes/no questions.

Panacéia or Azougue-de-Pobre

Names: Allheal (*Valeriana officinalis*). One of the names in Portuguese means "poor man's quicksilver."

Associations: Obaluaiê, Xangô.

Medicine: A powerful diuretic and effective measure against syphilis. It also can be added to the bath for skin diseases such as eczema, as well as rheumatism.

Uses: A sacred plant for all *ori* obligations.

Parietária or Alfavaca-de-Cobra

Names: Wall pellitory (*Parietaria officinalis* or *Monnieria trifolia*). The name in Portuguese means "snake's basil." This refers to any number of related climbing plants of the nettles family.

Associations: Obaluaiê, Oxum.

Medicine: The leaves are a diuretic for urinary tract and kidney infections. Apply a decoction of the leaves topically to skin irritations.

Uses: In spite of the fact that this plant belongs to the nettle family it does not sting on skin contact. It is an ingredient in many Umbanda spells, and is used in various abô and ori obligations.

Pau-D'Alho

Names: Garlic shrub (*Adenocalymna alliacea*). This climbing shrub smells like garlic.

Associations: Obaluaiê, Exu.

Medicine: Make a maceration of the leaves into a compress for skin tumors and hemorrhoids to relieve the pain. The leaves in a bath are also good for rheumatism and gonorrhea.

Uses: An ingredient of almost all ori obligations as well as baths that must be taken after purification rituals. The botanical is said to also purify domiciles and stores. It is thought to clear the air wherever money is exchanged. Garlic shrub is a key ingredient of strong purification baths because it removes Exu's influence from a person's path. To accomplish this, combine the botanical with California pepper and purple and white pine. The leaves also can be stuffed into poppets to perform image magick.

Piperegum Verde, Dracena, or Pau D'Água

Names: Dragon's blood resin (*Cordyline dracaena*) or copaiyé tree (*Vochysia thrysoidea*). One of the names in Portuguese means "water stick."

Associations: Oxum, Oxumarê, the Eguns, a primary axé of Oxóssi.

Medicine: Baths and compresses made from the leaves alleviate rheumatic pain.

Uses: Ori obligations; eliminates the influence of the Eguns from people or dwellings. In certain cases, this botanical has been used in emergency situations to remove the "hand" from the head of an initiate while the terreiro head is still alive. In the Afro-Brazilian occult herbals this plant is attributed with the ability to "surround things" and to "create frontiers."

Pitangueira

Names: Brazilian cherry (*Eugenia uniflora*). This small evergreen shrub has fragrant white flowers that give way to a crimson-colored edible fruit.

Association: Oxóssi.

Medicine: The tea helps rid children of roundworm.

Uses: Renowned for its ability to absorb negative fluids, this botanical is an ingredient of ori amacis, abô, bead washes, environmental incenses, and incenses to attract money.

To make a "wealthy way" incense, make a powder of the leaves with cinnamon powder, coffee powder, sugar, carnation flowers, and garlic straw. Burn the mixture outside the front door of your house or place of business. Leave the ashes outside until the following day, and dispose of them in a forest, on a beach, or in running water. In homage to Oxóssi, practitioners sometimes cut down a tree and place it in the terreiro as if it were planted there, and decorate it with fruit tied carefully to the branches.

Piteira

Names:	Century plant (*Agave americana*). This tropical plant has fleshy leaves and a tall, green-flowered stalk. It was formerly thought only to bloom every 100 years, hence the name.
Associations:	Ossãe, Obaluaiê.
Medicine:	An infusion of the green leaves disinfects wounds and dermatoses.
Uses:	The dried leaves are cut into small pieces and burned in personal purification incenses.

Sapê

Names:	Satintail.
Associations:	Exu, the Eguns.
Uses:	The roots are used for purification baths from the neck down. Satintail is also widely used for hut thatching.

Sumarê or Bisturi do Mato

Names:	*Cyrtopodium punctatum*. One of the names in Portuguese means "scalpel of the forest."
Associations:	Omulu and Oxóssi.

Medicine:	This orchid that is found growing on palms and other trees is more known to folk medicine than to magick because of its reputation to quickly open tumors and expel pus. It is a trusted anti-inflammatory. Scrape out the gum with a spoon and spread it on the inflamed part. The syrup made from the entire plant alleviates whooping and other persistent coughs.
Uses:	Baths, bead washes.

Urtiga-de-Mamão

Names:	Treadsoftly (*Cnidoscolus urens*).
Associations:	Obaluaiê, Omulu.
Medicine:	Helps improve the action of the kidneys and alleviates the pain from burns.
Uses:	Apply the dried leaves of this shrub with stinging spines, which lose their bite when dried in strong purification baths, from the neck down to drive away the Eguns.

Vassourinha-de-Igreja

Names:	Sweet broomwort (*Scoparia dulcis*).
Associations:	Oxum, Exu.
Uses:	In baths, purifies the body from the neck down from the influence of the Eguns. Together with cypress (one of Nanã's botanicals) and coastal straw (a plant sacred to Omulu), it frightens off the Eguns, Exu, and all evil.

FOODS OF THE GODS

AFRO-BRAZILIAN CUISINE

Afro-Brazilian cuisine is some of the most varied and delicious in the world. While based on African cooking, Brazilians take advantage of many different, delicious native ingredients and season their dishes to accommodate Brazilian tastes. Followers of Candomblé, in particular, exhibit the full range of their culinary talents when they offer their unique creations as gifts of sustenance to their gods.

abadô—Toasted corn. One of Omulu's favorite foods.

abará—A bean cake made with onion, salt, French beans, dendê, and sometimes shrimp, all wrapped in a banana leaf and cooked in a double boiler. This meal honors that famous couple, Xangô and Iansã.

aberém—A rice, bean, and sugar cake, stone-ground, wrapped in a banana leaf, tied with bark fiber, and steam cooked.

acaçá—Rice or corn flour mixed with salt and water. The mixture is cooked until it thickens, then wrapped in green banana leaves. Sometimes coconut milk and sugar are added.

acarajé—A round or oblong croquette made from grated French beans (previously soaked in water for three days to remove the shells), minced onion, and salt, then fried in dendê oil. Sometimes the center is filled with purée of dried shrimp and seasoned with onions and dried malagueta pepper. It is one of Iansã's favorite dishes.

acassá de fubá—Indian cornmeal cooked in water and wrapped in a banana leaf. This dish is accepted by almost all the Orixás.

adó or *adum*—Toasted ground corn mixed with dendê oil and bee honey. Oxum appreciates this meal.

afurá—A rice cake made with sugar.

agbê—A stew made from herbs and oil.

aguxô—A vegetable soup.

ajabó—Minced okra whipped with honey. It is one of Iroko's favorite dishes.

aluá—Rice or corn flour fermented with pineapple rinds and other fruit, then mixed with with grated ginger root, white or raw sugar, and lime. It is the preferred drink of many Orixás of the Caboclo Candomblés, especially Ogum. These days it is often substituted for champagne or wine.

amalá—A special kind of *caruru* made with okra sauce and manioc or rice flour mush. It is one of the Ibêji's favorite dishes. *Amalá de Ogum* is made from French beans, shrimp, and dendê oil, and is served at this Orixá's annual feast. *Amalá de Xangô* is prepared from pigeon breast or oxtail, okra, shrimp, and dendê oil.

ambrozo—Corn flour mixed with sugar.

anderé—A kind of *vatapá* made with French beans. Nanã likes this dish.

anju de fubá—Manioc flour paste eaten with shrimp and other shell-fish, fish, and meat.

aussá—Rice cooked in salt-free water, then beaten with a wooden spoon to a purée. Sometimes rice flour is added to give it the mushy consistency. Then it is fried into a cake with dendê oil. It is one of Oxum's special foods.

axoxô—Yellow corn mixed with coconut slices.

badofe—Shrimp with dendê oil.

balas and *bonbons*—Different kinds of candies and sweetmeats reserved for the Ibêji.

batêtê—Raw yam mixed with *epô* and salt.

bebida de Oxóssi—"Oxóssi's Drink" is made from fermented dendê and coconut. It is offered to this Orixá in a gourd with bee honey and a houseleek or an orange slice.

bobó—Yams and bee honey.

cachaça—Sugar cane, brandy, and white rum. When used for ritual purposes, it is often called *marafo*.

canjica—White or yellow corn cooked with salt.

caruru—Purée of different kinds of cooked herbs such as mustard grass, cat's claw, and pepper. It also often contains shrimp, fish, okra, pepper, lime, and dendê. The color is usually green. This favorite food of the Ibêji is served on their feast day.

conquém—Guinea hen. Besides being the dish of preference for many of the Orixás, the feathers are used in head-making rituals for the Iaôs. They are scattered over the blood that drips on the initiate's head.

dendê (*epo pupá* in Yoruba)—An orange-colored oil extracted from the *Elaeis guineensis*, or African palm tree, which is naturalized in Brazil. The oil is used to cook many Afro-Bahian dishes. The only Orixá who does not accept dendê is Oxalá.

denguê—Porridge made with white corn or rice cooked with sugar. It is a special food for Oxalá, Ogum, and Oxóssi.

doburu—Popcorn made in an iron pot over a wood fire or hot sand. Also called "Flowers of Omulu."

ebô—Porridge made from dried white corn cooked in vegetable oil and water. It is one of Oxalá's favorite dishes. Do not confuse the word with *ebó*, which is a sacrifice.

êcô—Corn porridge and raw sugar.

êcuru or *ecru-cu*—Cock or hen cooked for an axexê (the occasion of the death of a terreiro notable). It is served with a sweet concoction of which green corn paste is the chief ingredient. It is rolled in a banana leaf and baked.

êfô—A kind of *caruru* made from herbs such as mustard grass and bugloss.

êfum-ôguedê—Stone-mashed, dried banana.

farofa—Manioc flour fried in butter or oil; sometimes chopped beef jerky, onion, or eggs are added. Farofa accompanies bean, beef, or fowl dishes. If you can't get manioc flour, cream of rice from the box is a reasonable substitute.

feijoada—Brazil's national dish consisting of black beans cooked with organ meats, garlic, pepper, salt, and basil seasoning. It is served over rice with a side of cachaça and an orange slice.

French beans—A long-podded shell containing large, white beans.

fubá—Corn meal, Indian meal.

gronga—Whiskey with lime, ginger, and other herbs. (Another meaning of this word, "bad thing," is derived from the term *grongueiro*—a fake medium.)

guaraná—A very sweet soft drink made from the seeds of the native Brazilian shrub of the same name. It is loaded with caffeine, and is said to be an energizer and a diet pill. The makers of Pepsi are currently preparing to mass market this drink under another name in the United States.

gururu—The same as *doburu*, only this term is used when the dish is prepared for Oxumarê.

ibejuiri—Okra and dried fish with shrimp cooked in oil.

iché—Organs of sacrificed animals cooked in sweet oil.

ipeté—Cooked mashed yam seasoned with dendê oil, onion, pepper, and ground shrimp.

jurema—The hallucinogenic beverage made from the fruit, roots, and bark of this plant by the same name (*Pithecolobium tortum*).

kinana—Sesame, flour, salt, and sugar.

latipá—Food made with the wild mustard plant.

lelé—Carmelized, sweetened evaporated milk with ground coconut pieces. This is a favorite food of the female Orixás.

manjar do céu—Custard pudding.

meladinha—A drink made from sugar cane, brandy, and honey.

mi-ami-ami—Farofa fried in dendê and offered as a *despacho* to Exu so he will carry a petition to the Orixás.

moqueca—Fish or mussels simmered in olive or dendê oil with lime juice, vinegar, and pepper, and wrapped in a mango or tobacco leaf.

mungunzá (also spelled *mugunzá, munguzá*)—Dried white corn boiled in cow's milk and coconut milk and seasoned with cinnamon sugar.

oguede—Plantain fried in dendê oil.

olubô—Husked, finely chopped sun-dried manioc root. When ready to use, crush the pieces with a mortar and pestle, strain, and cover the ground manioc with boiling water.

omolucum—French beans and eggs seasoned with salt, grated shrimp, and dendê.

oxinxin—Fresh meat simmered with shrimp and dendê.

vatapá—Purée of fish and shrimp cooked in coconut milk and dendê and served with malagueta pepper. This orange-colored dish is eaten with *anju de fubá*.

uado—Pulverized popcorn mixed with bee honey or sugar and dendê. Offered to Oxóssi and Oxum.

xeketê—Hulled, toasted corn; powdered ginger; and raw sugar all fermented together.

xin-xin—Shredded chicken mixed with salt, garlic, and onion, and cooked in dendê. Serve to Iansã and Oxum.

FOODS OF THE ORIXÁS

Although variations exist among terreiros and traditions, the following dishes are among those offered most consistently to the Orixás. One day a year is set aside as if it were a birthday to honor each entity. On this annual feast day, special food is prepared for the entity and enjoyed by all.

Euá—Corn and coconut pieces, lelé.

Annual feast: various kinds of white foods.

Exu—Exu will eat almost anything, but his favorite foods are black cock and rooster, steak, popcorn, farofa cooked in dendê oil, lemon, lime, sugarcane liquor, cognac, champagne, efó.

Annual feast: acarajé, black and French beans, farofa cooked with corn and onion, roasted meat, wine, honey.

Iansã—Acarajé, squash, fish, shrimp, *xin-xin* of chicken, *ipeté*, fresh fish simmered in oil and seasoned with pepper, light beer, water from a waterfall, abará, pink mango.

Annual feast: acaçá with fourteen pieces of okra, white corn, French beans.

the Ibêji—Vatapá, bonbons, honey, apples, pears, grapes, *guaraná*, chicken.

Annual feast: caruru.

Iemanjá—White or green corn with sweet oil or honey; white hen and duck; she-goat stew; mullet simmered in oil and seaweed; manjar do céu; muqueca; sardines; shrimp; papaya.

Annual feast: rice, white anju, acaçá.

Iroko—Ajabó, white corn, French beans.

Annual feast: fried bananas, conquém, iché, acarajé, bonbons, honey.

Logun-Odê—Cock, pork chops and beans, various fruits, axoxó, omolocum.

Annual feast: white corn, yam, dendê oil.

Nanã—Anderé, mungunzá, acaçá, doburu, purple melons.

Annual feast: rice, yams, French beans, canjica, white corn.

Obá—Acarajé, amalá, abará.

Annual feast: French beans, farofa, eggs eaten with dendê oil.

Ogum—Amalá, red cock, goat, mushrooms, feijoada, organ meats, baked yams, potato, watercress, French beans cooked in dendê oil, sword mango, lager, aluá.

Annual feast: black beans, Amalá de Ogum, corn, rice.

Omulu—White cornmeal and bananas, cock, goat, corn flour, aberém, abadô, doburu, latipá, pineapple, orange.

Annual feast: farofa with dendê oil, rice, black beans, French beans.

Ossãe—Black beans, pork, farofa, honey, various fruits, tobacco.

Annual feast: rice, white corn, French beans, black beans, food made with dendê oil.

Oxalá—Anything white and without salt or dendê oil, including hen; plain Indian cornmeal; goat acacá of rice; mungunzá; canjica; aluá; denguê.

Annual feast: rice cooked with egg whites; ajabó; champagne.

Oxóssi—Axoxé, olubô, uado, jurema, various fruits, especially coconut xeketé, pork, red corn, peanuts, coconut, conquém.

Annual feast: French and black beans, rue, *abadô*, baked corn.

Oxum—Omolucum; adum; uado; muqueca of fish, meat, hen, chicken; aussá; xin-xin; lelé; banana; papaya; fresh spring water.

Annual feast: yams, cooked eggs, French beans, rice, corn with coconut.

Oxumarê—Gururu, aberém, beans, corn, rice, olive oil, acarajé, shrimp, tortoise.

Pomba-Gira—Raw *farofa de fubá*, pepper, onions, spoiled eggs, black hen or pigeon, dendê, coconut daiquiris, sugar cane liqueur, maracujá (a fruit), yam with cinnamon.

Xangô—Abará, caruru, adô, aberém, amalá of okra, all kinds of fruit, tortoise, amalá de Xangô, red cock, dark beer.

Annual feast: acarajé, black beans, *farofa*, rice.

MUSIC OF
THE SPHERES

adjá—A metal, one-, two-, three-, or four-clapper bell instrument used in many Umbanda and Candomblé ceremonies. In its best-known role, the mãe pequena holds it near a medium's ear and rings it to facilitate the trance state.

afofoê—A small, wooden flute; the only wind instrument brought to Brazil by Africans. It has fallen into disuse.

agogô—A rhythm instrument with two metal bells of slightly different sizes, which emit different sounds. The bells are either cylindrical or hexagonal, and are attached by a hoop. The agogô does not have a clapper; instead, it is played with a little metal stick.

agvdavi—The wooden drumsticks with which the drums are often played.

atabaques (also called *Ilus*)—Three different-sized ritual drums covered with hide and played with drumsticks or the hands. The drums initiate dances, invoke the entities, and welcome them as well as visiting Ogãs and other dignitaries to the terreiro.

cabaça—A bottle gourd that is the fruit of the *Cucurbita lagenaria* plant and other species. It is dried and emptied of its contents, then covered with a fiber net with capiá ("St. Mary's tears") seeds sewn on it. The rattle is shaken by a wooden handle. It is also called a *xeré*, when it is carried as Xangô's ritual instrument. It can also be called a *xaque-xaque*, *aguê*, or *afoxé* by some sects. The cabaça gourd can also be cut in half, painted, and used as a receptacle for food and drink of the Orixás.

caxixi—A kind of rattle that was used in Angolan traditions, but which appears rarely anymore.

ganzá—A rattle made from a metal box with little pebbles or lead pellets inside. It is used more in secular than in sacred music.

lê—The smallest of the three ritual drums.

palms—Clapping together the palms of the hands is a common way to mark the rhythm. This is especially practiced in funeral rites when the drums are not allowed to be played.

rum or *contra-run*—The largest of the three ritual drums.

rumpi—The middle-sized ritual drum.

terno—The set of ritual drums, made up of the small lê, the medium-sized rumpi, and the large rum or contra-run.

xaxará—A rattle that is the ritual musical instrument of Omulu. It is made from a bundle of straw tied into a sheath with cowrie shells or beads embroidered on it. This instrument represents plague and epidemic.

DRUMBEATS

adarúm—A quickening of the beat designed to induce the Orixás to descend.

aderé—Oxum's and Iemanjá's drumbeat.

agueré—Oxóssi's and Iansã's drumbeat.

alujá—Xangô's drumbeat.

barravento—A drumbeat that will serve any Orixá.

bravun—Oxalá's drumbeat.

egô—Another of Iansã's drumbeats.

ibi—Another of Oxalá's drumbeats.

opanijé—Omulu's drumbeat.

saté—Oxumarê's drumbeat (also the *Jikâ*).

GLOSSARY
OF TERMS

Portuguese, Yoruba, and potentially unfamiliar English terms that occur in the text are defined here. See Appendix D for names of foods and Appendix E for musical instruments.

abebé—A round, symbolic fan. Iemanjá's is made from silver embossed with the figure of a fish or a mermaid. Oxum's is fashioned from brass with a star etched in the center.

abiã—Aspirant to mediumship.

abô—Ritual purification bath given at the time of initiation.

adê—Beaded metal or silk crown worn by most of the female Orixás in their particular colors.

adjá—Bell used in rituals, for among other reasons, as an aid in trancework.

alá—A white canopy placed over the altar in some ceremonies.

alubaça—Onion, as used in one kind of yes\no divination.

amaci—Head bath, the purpose of which is to strengthen the bond between the medium and his/her head Orixá; also a bead bath.

Amado, Jorge—Bahian fiction writer who wove Candomblé rituals into his works, many of which have been translated into English.

Angola—Southwest African region that lies along the Atlantic coast, and is inhabited by the Bantu linguistic group and people.

área—Literally the "area" off the kitchen where maids do laundry and perform household chores.

assentamento—Representation of an Orixá's power. It is also known as a fetish and can include a stone, shell, tree, or metal object,

axé—Life force. The power of the Orixás.

axexê—Funeral rite for a terreiro notable.

Axogum (**or** *Axogun*)—Chief animal sacrificer.

Babá—Ancestral spirit of the Egun cult.

Baba-Iaô—Male spiritual leader and priest of Ifá. No traditional Baba-Iaôs exist anymore in Brazil, but out of reverence, the term is used to denote a Babalorixá.

Babalorixá—Male spiritual leader.

Bahia—Southern northeast state of Brazil. Also refers to the capital of the state, Salvador, Bahia, where many people of African descent settled, and which is known as the "Rome of Africa."

balé—House of the Eguns.

banda—Group of rituals, literally a "band."

banho de descarga—Purification bath, literally a "discharge bath."

Bantu—People, tribes, and languages belonging to the large linguistic group of 300 dialects including Kimbundo and Kikongo. The area of Bantu influence covers two-thirds of black Africa, including Angola and the Congo.

barracão—Main salon of the terreiro where public ceremonies take place.

bater cabeça—To bow by touching one's forehead to the ground before the spiritual leader, visiting dignitaries, and the drums during a ceremony in a gesture of obeisance.

Batuque—Generic name for Nagô-Pajelança-influenced cults. A kind of African dance performed to atabaques.

búzio (*Cyproea moneta*)—A small, yellowish white, oval cowrie-conch shell with one rounded side and another serrated side. The shell is used in divination, decoration, and as an offering to the gods.

Caboclo—A perfected ancestral spirit of a dead Mestizo who returns to earth in the terreiros to aid humanity. From a Portuguese term meaning "red-skinned."

cachaça—Alcoholic drink similar to rum and made from fermented sugarcane.

camarinha—Chamber where the future initiate is sequestered. Also known as a roncó.

Cambone—Assistant to the spiritual leader.

Candomblé—Brazilianized African religion including Gegê, Sudanese, and Bantu rituals.

carrego—Bundle of personal effects belonging to a dead parishoner.

casa de santo—Shop that sells religious supplies for the various popular sects.

Catimbó—Amerindian religion with strong influence from African sects, Catholicism, and Spiritism.

centro—Another word for a terreiro, or place of worship.

chakras—Centers of the body that align with the central nervous column. Power is thought to flow into these centers from the cosmos and radiate outward. Chakras are said to influence health and natural development.

charity session—Ceremony in which the entities incorporate through mediums in order to give advice and healing to clients.

compadre—Godfather; good friend.

Congo—People and religious sects that come from a large area of equatorial Africa that is bordered by Angola. Many slaves from this region were brought to Rio, Recife, and Maranhão.

contra-Egun—Braided straw armband tightly bound to the body to ward off the Eguns during axexê ceremonies.

Curandeiro—Herbalist who cures illnesses by using a mixture of botanicals and prayers to the gods.

curiador—Drink for an Orixá or other entity.

curimba—Afro-Brazilian religious song that honors the divinities and other entities.

Dã—Sacred serpent of Benin, Africa represented by a snake swallowing its tail.

Dagã—Guardian of the house of Exu.

de Freitas, João—Theological writer who authored the first book about Umbanda.

defumação—Smoking with tobacco and other herbs to rid the body of evil spirits.

de Morais, Zélio—Founder of the first modern terreiro in Rio de Janeiro.

dendê—Polysaturated orange oil that comes from the fruit of the *Elaeis guineensis* palm and is widely used in Afro-Brazilian cuisine.

doburu—Sand-popped corn offering to Omulu and other Orixás.

Dudu Calunga—Ossãe's one-legged companion with musical talent.

Ebâmi—Female initiate with seven years of experience.

Egun—Soul of a dead African ancestor who returns to earth in the terreiro. Some Eguns are evolved, others are backward and need to be controlled.

Ekédi—Festival organizer and assistant to the Iaôs.

elemental—Spirit creature that typifies one of the four elements. Elementals feed on human energy and are difficult to control.

Encantado—Orixá represented by a Caboclo in the Amerindian sects. The word in Portuguese means "Enchanted One."

"Eri ieiê ô!"—Salutation to Oxum.

Euá—In some terreiros she is a water nymph, in others, she is a war goddess, still in others she is the cobra sister of Oxumarê who represents beauty as symbolized by the light band of the rainbow.

Exi-de-orixá—A first-degree male initiate.

Exu—Universal agent of magick and messenger of the gods. Sometimes he is considered a devil.

fechar a cabeça—Ceremony in which a medium's spirit guide prevents the person from ever again incorporating an Orixá. From the Portuguese phrase meaning "to close the head."

figa—Talismanic figure of a fist with the thumb protruding between the first and second fingers.

filá—Long, fringed, straw hood decorated with cowrie shells. It covers most of the body. One of Omulu's symbols.

filho-de-santo—From the Portuguese phrase meaning "son/daughter of the saint." A cult member or initiate of the sect.

Flowers of Omulu—Omulu's sacred hot sand-popped corn.

Gegê—General name for slaves who came from the ancient region of Dahomey. The Fon dialect of the Ewe language.

grau de sandice—From Portuguese, "grain of insanity." A bit of craziness.

guaraná—A sweet, carbonated drink made from the plant by the same name. A favorite beverage of the Ibêji.

guia—Colored beads of a medium's head Orixá, which are worn when the person is in a trance; also worn at other times to identify the medium's head Orixá. The word is also another name for one's holy guardian angel.

Hana-Noka—A kind of stick incense alleged to bring harmony to the environment.

head making—Initiation ceremony, the purpose of which is to bind the medium to his/her chief Orixá.

head Orixá—A cult member's principal Orixá and guardian angel.

Iabassê—Chief cook of food for the Orixás and public functions.

Iyá Kalá, Iyá Detá, and *Iyá Nassó*—Three Nigerian Xangô priestesses who founded the first terreiro in Salvador, Bahia.

Ialaxé—Guardian of the terreiro's axés.

Ialorixá—Female spiritual leader.

Iansã—Goddess of wind and the tempest.

Iaô—Priestess or initiated medium who is also called a "bride of the Orixás."

Iá Tebexê—Female song leader.

the Ibêji—Twin Orixás who represent the principle of duality.

ibiri—Symbolic straw broom belonging to Nanã.

Iemanjá—Goddess of the ocean and of the Ogun river in Africa. Considered the mother of all the Orixás.

Ifá—God of the ineffable and divination, sometimes syncretized with the Holy Ghost.

incorporation—Spirit possession of a medium while in trance.

Iroko—White fig tree god (*Ficus doliaria*).

iruexim—Horsetail whip belonging to Iansã with which she controls the Eguns.

ixã—Black-and-white-striped cane used to control the Eguns.

jogo de búzios—Divination technique that uses cowrie shells thrown in a circle to tell the future.

Jurema—Female Cabocla around whom a cult has grown. Also the *Pithtecolobium tortum* tree, which renders a hallucinogenic drink.

juremação—A rite of initiation for members of the Jurema sect.

Juremados—Entities who descend into the bodies of mediums who have ingested the hallucinogenic jurema plant.

Kardec, Allan—French nineteenth-century founder of Spiritism.

Kekerê—Chief assistant to the spiritual leader. Also known as a "little mother" or "little father."

Keto—Ancient West African kingdom around the Nigerian-Benin border. People were transported in large numbers from this region to Bahia where they continued to practice their old religion, which still influences Candomblé.

kora—The enchanted harp played by Dudu Calunga.

"Kosi ewe kosi orisà"—A proverb meaning "Without leaves the Orixás cannot exist; without leaves there is no axé."

Logun-Edê—Young god of fishermen and the hunt. Sometimes confused with his father Oxóssi.

Macumba—Brazilian religion similar to Quimbanda and Umbanda primarily centered in Rio and adjoining states.

Macumbeiro—Practitioner of Macumba.

mãe—Mother.

mão-de-faca—Special preparation and instruction to the Axogum, which enables him to sacrifice. Portuguese for "knife-hand."

mãe-de-santo—Portuguese for "mother of the saint." Also known as an Ialorixá.

mãe pequena—Chief female assistant. Also known as an Iá-Kekerê.

mandinga—Kind of enchantment often associated with the Pretos Velhos.

nação—Group of rituals of a particular sect.

Nagô—Brazilian word for people of Yoruba origin and the rituals they practice.

Nanã—Grandmother of the gods. The oldest water goddess.

Obá—Goddess of the Nigerian river by the same name.

Obaluaiê—Omulu as a young man.

obi—Kola nut used in divination to answer yes\no questions.

odu—Configuration of cowrie shells that holds the secret to the future.

ofá—Wooden, metal, or bronze bow and arrow that is Oxóssi's symbol.

Ogã—Patron of the terreiro.

Ogã-Alakê—Drummer who may also play other musical instruments. Also known as the Ogã de Tambor or Ogã-Nilo.

Ogã-Beré—A new Ogã.

Ogã-Calofé—Head drummer.

Ogê—Leaders of the cults of the Eguns. Also known as an Anixa.

ogn—Honey.

Ogum—God of war, agriculture, martial arts, protection, and responsibility.

ojá—White shawl used as a turban or a covering for the chest.

Olórun—Supreme creator god of the Yoruba people. Also known as Zambi.

Omulu—God of pestilence, disease, and death.

opelê de Ifá—Mode of divination that uses a metal necklace strung with nuts.

Orixá—A god or goddess of the Afro-Brazilian pantheon.

Ossãe—God of botanicals and medicine.

ossé—Animal sacrifice.

otá—Sacred stone of an Orixá.

Oxaguiã—The young Oxalá.

Oxalá—Creator god of humanity.

Oxalufã—The elder Oxalá.

oxê—Xangô's symbol, a wooden cane topped by a double-edged ax.

Oxóssi—God of the hunt and forest.

Oxum—Goddess of sweet water, wealth, and beauty. Goddess of the Oxum river in Nigeria.

Oxumarê—Snake god and god of the rainbow and good weather.

Oyó—Region and city in Nigeria that was the capital of the ancient Yoruba empire. Also the rituals that are from this area.

padê—Offering to Exu.

pai—Father.

pai-de-santo—Portuguese for "father of the saint." Also known as a Babalorixá.

pai pequeno—Chief male assistant. Also known as a Babá Kekerê.

pajé—Indian witch doctor and shaman.

Pajelança—Amerindian sect that mixes in Spiritism and Roman Catholicism. It is popular in Amazon and Piauí states.

passe—Laying on of the hands, but without touching the body of the patient, with the intent to heal.

peji—Altar for the Orixás where their food, symbols, fetishes, et cetera are kept.

Peji-Gã—Terreiro caretaker and organizer of public festivals.

pemba—Ritual chalk with which invocations and other signs and sigils are drawn.

pilão—Pestle and symbol of Oxalá and Ossãe.

Pomba-Gira—Female counterpart of Exu.

ponto cantado—Invocational song.

ponto riscado—A sigil scratched on the ground or on an object, often with a pemba.

pó pupa—Dendê oil.

Preto Velho—A perfected ancestral spirit of an old Black slave who returns to earth in the terreiros to aid humanity.

Quimbanda—Popularly considered to be the "dark side" of Umbanda. Adherents follow African traditions.

quitute—Afro-Brazilian delicacy often sold on the street to raise money for the terreiro.

roncó—The cell where future initiates are sequestered. Also known as a camarinha.

"Salve!"—"Greetings!"

"Saravá!"—"Hail!"

Sidagã—The Dagã's helper.

sertão—Dry grassland desert of the interior of the northeast region of Brazil.

Seu—"Mister"; a term of affectionate respect.

sigil—Occult symbol that represents a spirit or other entity.

Spiritism—Religion founded in nineteenth century and based on spirit communication, the doctrines of which deeply affects the Afro-Brazilian sects.

syncretism—Intermingling and fusion of the characteristics of deities of different religions.

terreiro—Locale where rituals take place. From the Portuguese word meaning "large, flat, clear piece of land."

tombo—Official loss of the privilege of mediumship.

Tupí—Brazilian Indian tribe and language.

Umbanda—Brazilian religion that combines precepts from Spiritism, Candomblé, Positivism, Roman Catholicism, and Amerindian sects.

Vodunsi—An honored initiate with at least thirty years of experience in the Gegê-Nagê tradition.

Vodunsi-hunjai—New initiate in the Gegê tradition.

Western Magickal Mystery Tradition—Accumulation of occult knowledge from Occidental mystery traditions, including those of the Gnostic Ceremonial Magicians, Egyptians, Greeks, Celts, Norse, and others.

Witchcraft (Wicca)—A nature-based New Age religion that relies on Western European rituals of a rich, long oral tradition.

Xampanã—The elder Omulu in his destructive mode.

Xangô—God of thunder, lightning, and justice. An African-Amerindian religion of northeast Brazil.

Xavier, Chico—Spiritist medium who contacted the dead using automatic writing.

Yoruba—Sudanese people from Nigeria and the regions of West Africa that extend from Lagos. Because of their high culture and numerical superiority, they were influential on Brazilian culture and religion.

Zambi—Supreme creator god of the Bantu and Umbanda cults. Another name for Olórun.

BIBLIOGRAPHY

WORKS IN ENGLISH

Alves Neto, Antonio Teixeira. *Pomba-Gira: Rituals to Invoke the Formidable Powers of the Female Messenger of the Gods.* Trans. Carol L. Dow. Burbank, Calif.: Technicians of the Sacred, 1990.

Bramly, Serge. *Macumba: The Teachings of Maria-José, Mother of the Gods.* Trans. Meg Bogin. New York: St. Martin's Press, 1977.

Brown, Diana De Groat. *Umbanda: Religion and Politics in Urban Brazil.* Ann Arbor, Mich.: UMI Research Press, 1986.

Brumana, Fernando Giotellina and Elda González Martínez. *Spirits from the Margin: Umbanda in São Paulo, A Study of Popular Religion and Social Experience.* Uppsala, Sweden: Almqvis and Wihiell International, 1989.

Drury, Nevill. *Dictionary of Mysticism and the Occult.* San Francisco: Harper and Row, 1985.

Freyre, Gilberto. *The Masters and the Slaves: A Study in the Development of Brazilian Civilization.* Trans. Samuel Putnam. New York: Putman's, 1946.

Ireland, Rowan. *Kingdoms Come: Religion and Politics in Brazil.* Pittsburgh, Penn.: University of Pittsburgh Press, 1991.

Kent, R.K. "Palmares: An African State in Brazil." *Journal of African Studies,* 6:2 (1965): 161–175.

Langguth, A. J. *Macumba.* New York: Harper and Row, 1975.

Leacock, Seth and Ruth Leacock. *Spirits of the Deep: A Study of Afro-Brazilian Cults.* New York: 1972.

Levine, Robert M. *Historical Dictionary of Brazil. Latin American History Dictionary No. 19.* Metuchen, N.J.: The Scarecrow Press, Inc., 1979.

Melville, J. and Frances S. Hershovits, eds. *Afro-Bahian Religious Songs from Brazil: Songs of the African Cult Groups.* Washington, D.C.: Library of Congress, Music Division, Folk Music of the Americas, n.d. (This is a pamphlet that accompanies a music tape cassette.)

St. Clair, David. *Drum and Candle.* New York: Doubleday, 1971.

Thompson, Robert Farris. *Face of the Gods: Art and Altars of Africa and the African Americas.* New York: The Museum for African Art, 1993.

Wafer, Jim. *The Taste of Blood: Spirit Possession in Brazilian Can-domblé*. Philadelphia: University of Pennsylvania Press, 1991.

Warren, Donald, Jr. "The Negro and Religion in Brazil." *Race*, 6:3 (1965).

——— "Portuguese Roots of Brazilian Spiritism." *Luso-Brazilian Review*, 5:2 (December1968): 3–34.

WORKS IN PORTUGUESE

Alves Neto, Antonio Teixeira. *Curas, Mandingas e Feitiços de Preto-Velho*. 4th ed. Rio de Janeiro: Editora Eco, n.d.

Anon. *1500 Pontos Riscados na Umbanda*. Vol. II. Rio de Janeiro: Editora Eco, n.d.

Bandeira, Raimundo Cavalcanti. *O Que É a Umbanda?* Rio de Janeiro: Editora Eco, 1973.

Barcellos, Mário César. *Os Orixás e o Segredo da Vida: Lógica, Mitologia e Ecologia*. Rio de Janeiro: Pallas, 1991.

Barreto, Paulo (aka João do Rio). *As Religiões no Rio*. Rio de Janeiro: Editora Nova Aguilar, S.A., 1976.

Bastide, Roger. *O Candomblé da Bahia: Rito Nagô*. São Paulo: Editora Nacional, Cia., 1978.

———. *Estudos Afro-Brasileiros*. São Paulo: Editora Perspectiva, 1973.

———. *As Religiões Africanas no Brasil*. São Paulo: Livraria e Editora Primeira, 1971.

Cacciatore, Olga Gudolle. *Dicionário de Cultos Afro-Brasileiros*. Rio de Janeiro: Forense Universitária/SEEC, 1977.

Cantuária, Claúdia Maria. *Feitiços para o Amor*. 2nd. ed. Rio de Janeiro: Editora Eco, n.d.

Carneiro, Edison. *Candomblés da Bahia*. Salvador: Ministério do Estado, Secretária de Educação e Saúde, 1948.

———. *Decimália: Os Cultos de Origem Africana no Brasil*. Rio de Janeiro: Ministério da Educação e Cultura, 1959.

———. *O Quilombo dos Palmares*. Rio de Janeiro: Editora Civilização Brasileira, 1966.

Cupertino, Fausto. *As Muitas Religiões do Brasileiro*. Rio de Janeiro: Civilização Brasileira, 1976.

Decelso. *Babalaôs e Ialorixás*. 2nd ed. Rio de Janeiro: Editora Eco, n.d.

———. Umbanda de Caboclos. 3rd ed. Rio de Janeiro: Editora Eco, 1967.

de Freitas, Byron Torres, and Wladimir Cardoso de Freitas. *Na Gira da Umbanda e das Almas*. 4th ed. Rio de Janeiro: Editora Eco, n.d.

Farelli, Ana Lúcia. *Iemanjá*. Rio de Janeiro: Editora Eco, n.d.

Feijó, Atenéia. "O Despertar dos Magos." *Manchete*, 23 July, 1977: 66–76.

———. "Umbanda." *Gente*, May 1977: 96–107.

Gomes, Vera Braga de Souza. *O Ritual da Umbanda: Fundamentos Esotéricos*. Rio de Janeiro: Editora Tecnoprint, S.A., 1989.

Itaoman, Mestre. *Pemba: A Grafia Sagrada dos Orixás*. Brasília: Thesaurus, 1990.

Kardec, Allan. *O Evangelho Segundo o Espiritismo*. Trans. J. Herculano Pires. 13th ed. São Paulo: LAKE, 1977.

———. *O Principiante Espírita*. 12th ed. Rio de Janeiro: Federação Espírita Brasileira, 1955.

———. *Introdução ao Estudo da Doutrina Espírita.* Trans. Guillón Ribeiro. Rio de Janeiro: Federação Espírita Brasileira, 1946.

———. *O Livro dos Médiuns.* São Paulo: LAKE, 1975.

Lacerda, Ariomar. *Yemanjá: A Rainha do Mar.* 2nd ed. Rio de Janeiro: Pallas, 1989.

Lucius. *Oxalá.* 2nd ed. Rio de Janeiro: Editora Eco, n.d.

Luz, Marco Aurélio and Georges Lapassade. *O Segredo da Macumba.* Rio de Janeiro: Editora Paz e Terra, S.A., 1972.

Morgan, René. *Enciclopédia das Ervas e Plantas Medicinais.* São Paulo: Hermes Editôra, Ltda., n.d.

Nery, Marina. "A Magia dos Orixás." Manchete, December 1, 1990: 40–47.

Oderigo, Néstor Ortiz. *Macumba: Culturas Africanas en el Brasil.* (In Spanish.) Buenos Aires: Plus Ultra, 1975.

Ogã Gimbereuá. *Ebós: Feitiços no Candomblé.* Rio de Janeiro: Editora Eco, n.d.

Pinto, Altair. *Dicionário da Umbanda.* 3rd ed. Rio de Janeiro: Editora Eco, n.d.

Portugal, Afra Guedos. *O Poder do Candomblé: Com Aspectos da Religiosidade dos Gantois.* Rio de Janeiro: Editora Tecnoprint, S.A., 1986.

Portugal, Fernandes. *Axé: Poder dos Deuses Africanos.* Rio de Janeiro: Editora Eco, n.d.

———. *Encanto e Magia dos Orixás no Candomblé.* Rio de Janeiro: Editora Tecnoprint, S.A., 1986.

———. *Curso da Língua Yoruba.* Rio de Janeiro: Centro de Estudos e Pesquisas de Cultura Yoruba, 1981.

Possera de Eufrázio, Pompílio. *Catecismo do Umbandista.* 6th ed. Rio de Janeiro: Editora Eco, 1974.

Ramos, Arthur. *O Negro na Civilização Brasileira.* Rio de Janeiro: Livraria Editora Casa do Estudante do Brasil, 1956.

Ribeiro, José. *Cerimônias da Umbanda e do Candomblé.* 2nd ed. Rio de Janeiro: Editora Eco, 1974.

———. *Comidas de Santo e Oferendas.* 12th ed. Rio de Janeiro: Editora Eco, n.d.

———. *O Jogo de Búzios.* 6th ed. Rio de Janeiro: Pallas, 1990.

———. *O Poder das Ervas na Umbanda.* 2nd ed. Rio de Janeiro: Editora Eco, n.d.

Sales, Nívio Ramos. *Receitas de Feitiços e Encantos Afro-Brasileiros.* Rio de Janeiro: Achiamé, 1982.

Serrano, Geraldo. *Ogum.* 2nd ed. Rio de Janero: Editora Eco, n.d.

———. *Omulú: O Médico dos Pobres.* 4th ed. Rio de Janeiro: Editora Eco, 1982.

———. *Oxóssi.* Rio de Janeiro: Editora Eco, n.d.

Valente, Aurélio A. *Sessões Práticas e Doutrinárias do Espiritismo.* 5th ed. Rio de Janeiro: Federação Espírita Brasileira, 1938.

Varanda, Jorge Alberto. *Os Eguns do Candomblé.* Rio de Janeiro: Editora Eco, n.d.

Verger, Pierre. *Orixás: Deuses Ioruba na África e no Novo Mundo.* São Paulo: Editora Corrupio, 1981.

Wantuil, Zeus. *Grandes Espíritos do Brasil: 53 Biografias.* 2nd ed. São Paulo: Federação Espírita Brasileira, 1969.

INDEX

abiã, 96

abô, 159, 162, 165, 190–191, 196, 198, 203, 206–207, 210–211

adjá, 80–81, 222

African, xiii, 7–9, 12–13, 16–17, 19–22, 44, 46, 53, 74–76, 87–88, 92, 119, 121, 129, 136, 138, 146, 171–172, 177–178, 183, 188, 214, 217

Afro-Bahian, 103, 105, 112

alá, 125, 138

Alagoas, 17, 74, 185

Alibá, 73

alubaça, 134

amaci, 124–125, 148, 160, 166

Amado, Jorge, 5, 105

Amerindian, xii, 5, 8–9, 14, 16–17, 19, 87, 121, 127, 130, 171, 205

Angola, 8, 12, 193

Angolan-Congolese, 17, 19

Aryan, 121

assentamentos, 22, 72, 79, 95

astral administration, 127

aum-bandhu, 8

axé, 19, 21–23, 25, 27, 29, 31, 33, 35–39, 41, 43, 45, 47–48, 78–80, 92, 95, 108–109, 138, 150, 155, 207, 211

axexê, 69–70

Axogun (Axogum), 84, 86, 106

axoxô, 102, 216

Babá-Kekerê, 80, 85, 95

Babalâo (*see also* Babalorixá), 95

Babalorixá, 11, 85, 89, 91, 95, 106, 131, 133, 205

Bahia, 4–5, 12, 20, 41, 70, 105, 119

balê, 71–72

bandas, 9

banhos de descarga (*see also* discharge baths), 160

Bantu, 12, 22, 129, 193

Bara, 52

Barcellos, Mario César, 55–56, 74, 109, 136

barracão, 85, 92, 97, 104

Bastide, Roger, 19

bater cabeça, 10

Batuques, 65, 76

Bem, Jorge, 5

black magick, 14, 19, 53, 101, 110, 116, 128, 195, 200

Blavatsky, Madame Helena Petrovna, 76

Book of Mediums, The, 6

Book of Spirits, The, 6

Brown, Diana De Groat, 87, 96

cabana, 91

Caboclas, 76, 128

 Sereia do Mar, 76

Cabocla Jurema, 65–67, 123

Caboclos, 3, 17, 62–65, 67, 75–76, 124, 127–128, 132, 141–142, 156–157, 163, 165, 183, 192, 195, 198

 Araribóia, 75

 Arranca-Toco, 123

 Arranda, 75

 Cobra Coral, 75

 Estrela do Mar, 76

 Guiné, 76

 lines/ sects/traditions, 12–13, 20, 105, 130

 Malembá, 76

 Pedra Branca, 75

 Pena Branca, 76

 Sete Encruzilhadas (Seven Cross-roads), 9, 76

 Sol e Lua, 75

 Treme-Terra, 63, 76

 Vento, 76

 Uytán, 147

cachaça, 50, 52, 66, 99–100, 102, 105, 193

camarinha, 84, 93, 97

Cambone (Cambona, Cambono), 81–82, 85, 95

Candomblé, xii, 2, 5, 8–9, 12–14, 19–20, 23, 55, 69–70, 76, 80, 84–85, 87–88, 91, 96–97, 125, 127, 138, 159, 168, 207–208

canjica, 100–101

cantigas, 137

carrego, 71–72

Casa Branca de Engenho Velho, 91

casas de santo, 3

Catimbó, 2, 20, 65, 187, 205

Celts, 47, 108, 188

centros, 11, 88, 91, 105, 140, 163

Ceremonial Magick, xii, 187

 Ceremonial Magicians, 126

Christian, 14, 35, 108

Collor, Fernando, 110

compadre, 52

Congo, 12, 51, 74, 193

contra-Egun, 71

cowrie shell (*see also* jogo de búzios), 13, 16, 41–43, 50–51, 59, 72, 79, 95, 104, 106, 112, 115, 131–132, 134, 136, 159, 163, 180–182, 184–185

the Craft, *see* Witchcraft

Cupertino, Fausto, 18
curandero, 16
curiadores, 105
curimba, 67, 76

Dã, 43
Dagã, 82, 96, 107
de Alencar, José, 75
de Freitas, Joao, 9
de Morais, Zélio, 9
defumações, 16
Deliberative Council of Umbanda, 11, 19
dendê, 66, 83, 95, 100, 104, 107, 134, 199, 207
Denizard (see also Kardec, Allan and Rivail, Hippolite-León), 5
despacho, 137
Dictionary of Afro-Brazilian Cults, The (Diconário de Cultos Afro-Brasileiros), 130, 138
dictatorship, 15, 30, 110, 168
Doctrine of Signatures, 126
Dom Pedro II, Emperor, 6
Dona Flor and Her Two Husbands, 5, 105
Dudu Calunga, 39

Ebâme, 83, 96
Eguns, 16, 24, 33, 44, 64, 68, 70–73, 76, 163, 178, 188–189, 191, 195, 197, 203, 211–213
Egyptian, 121, 126, 128
Ekéde, 82, 91, 96
elementals, 22, 142
encantados (Enchanted Ones), 16, 20
encanto, 137
Espirito Santo, 129
Esquivel, Laura, 105
Euá, 38, 46
Exus, 3, 13–14, 16, 19, 25, 27–28, 41–42, 48, 50–59, 72, 74, 82, 92–93, 99–101, 106–107, 111, 116, 120,
123, 127, 130, 132, 137, 145, 150, 156–157, 161, 188, 191–194, 196–204, 207–208, 210, 212–213
Arranca-Toco, 74–75
baptized Exu, 58
Brasa, 74
Capa Preta, 74
Caveira, 52, 74
Cheiroso, 74
Cobra Coral, 74
Elegbara, 52, 74, 197
Exu Line, 50, 130
Exu of the Souls, 51
Mangueira, 74, 208
Marabô, 52, 74
Meia-Noite, 74
pagan Exu
Sete Catacumbas, 74
Sete Encruzilhadas (Seven Cross-roads) 51, 55, 74, 99–101
seven Exus, 50, 52
Tiriri, 74
Tranca-Ruas, 51, 74, 132
personal sigil, 123
Veludo, 74

farofa, 100, 107
farofa de dendê, 100
fechar a cabeça, 11
feitiço, 137
filá, 32, 73, 182
filha-de-santo, 48, 70
filha, 82
filho-de-santo, 23, 48, 79–80, 86

Gabriela Clove and Cinnamon, 105
Gegê, 12, 47, 70, 84
Gilberto, Gil, 5
Gnostic, 121
Gomes, Vera Braga de Souza, 14, 19, 75, 127, 138
Gospel According to Spiritism, The, 6

Greek, 189, 192

guaraná, 66, 112

guias, 103, 124-125, 132, 134-135, 137, 159, 177-185

guiame, 137

Guinea, 51, 74, 76, 115, 158–159, 163, 203

Hana-Noka, 155

head-making, 82–84, 156

Iá Kekerê, 84

Iá Tebexê, 83, 96

Iabassê, 83, 96, 103–104

Ialaxé, 81, 95

Ialorixá, 11, 69, 79, 93, 95, 148, 205

Iansã, 24–25, 40–41, 47, 68, 76, 120, 125, 128, 132, 150, 156, 178, 185, 189–190, 195, 203, 206

Iaôs, 80, 82–85, 91, 96, 202

Ibêji, the, 25–26, 112, 120, 122, 156, 179

Iemanjá, 26–28, 33, 35–36, 76, 91, 101, 113, 120, 125, 128, 132–133, 156, 158, 160, 179, 193, 199, 206

Iemanjá Day, 23, 101

Ifá, 38, 48, 79, 91, 95, 131, 133–134, 152, 199

Ikê, Ibó, Ibú, 73

incorporation, 5, 10–11, 23, 25, 28, 33, 43, 60–61, 73, 81–82, 91, 97, 105, 124, 128, 140, 163, 165

incorporated entity, 61

Indians, 16, 62–63, 65, 75, 87, 187

Iroko, 47, 190, 205

iruexim, 24, 178

Itaoman, Mestre, 136–137

Iyá Kalá, Iyá Detá, Iyá Nassó, 12

Judaism, 2, 89, 108

Judeo-Christian, 107

jugo de búzios (see also cowrie shells), 131, 134

Jurema (see also Cabocla Jurema), 65–67, 158, 186–187

personal sigil, 123

jurema tree (Pithecolobium tortum), 20, 47, 187

juremação, 66

juremados, 66

Kardec, Allan (see also Denizard and Rivail, Hippolite-León), 5–6, 9, 129

Kardecist, 91

Keto, 12

Kikongo, 12, 19

kimbanda, 8

kimbudu, 19

kora, 40

Lapassade, Georges, 20

Laroiê, 52, 132

Law of Umbanda, 10, 28, 67

legions, 9, 58, 64, 91, 125, 127–129, 137, 139

Legions of the Mermaids, 128

Like Water for Chocolate, 105

lines (of vibration), 7, 9–10, 19, 30, 50, 56, 64, 72–76, 79, 118, 120–121, 124–130, 133, 152, 157, 187

African Line, 129

Aiahuasca Line, 130

Black Line, 130

Line of Ogum, 64, 74, 128

Line of Oxalá, 128

Line of Oxóssi, 64, 75

Line of the Caboclos, 124

Line of the Souls, 72–73, 129–130, 157

Mixed Line, 130

Mosurabi Line, 130

Nagô Line, 130

Oriental Line, 120, 128, 130

Quimbanda lines, 130

Skeleton Line, 130

Whilte Line of Umbanda, 129–130, 187

Logun-Odê, 25, 38, 47

Loko (*see also* Iroko), 47

Luz, Marco Aurélio, 20

Macumba, xii, 2, 5, 8, 14–15, 19–20, 23, 88–89, 96, 110, 125, 157, 161

mãe pequena, 95

mãe-de-santo, 48, 69–70, 95, 161

magi, 13, 68, 126, 128

magnetizer, 120, 164

Majebajó, 73

mandingas, 60

mao de faca, 86

medium, 2, 4, 6–7, 10–11, 18, 20, 23, 25, 28, 33, 40, 42–43, 46, 48, 60–62, 68, 71, 73, 80–84, 89, 91–92, 97, 102, 108, 119–121, 124, 128, 137, 139, 141–143, 146, 148, 152, 154–155, 157, 159–161, 163–165, 190–191, 203

Messainism, 167

Minas Gerais, 19, 129

munguzaná, 116

Nagô, 12, 76

Nanã, 28–30, 33, 35–36, 38, 43, 46, 48, 76, 128, 133, 135, 150, 180, 201, 207, 213

National Deliberative Council, 19

Nigeria, 12

Norse, 108

northeast, 4–5, 12, 17, 64, 96, 167, 197–198, 202

Nunes, Atila, 4

Obaluaiê, 25, 32, 38, 130, 181, 190, 193–194, 196, 198, 200, 208–210, 212–213

obi, 134, 209

Odé, 38

Ogã, 85, 96

  Ogã Alaké, 85

  Ogã Calofé, 85, 104

ogn, 83

Ogum, 25, 27, 29–32, 37, 59, 64, 74, 91–92, 94, 113, 120, 122, 129–130, 132, 145, 150, 154, 156, 160, 181, 185, 191, 193, 200–201, 204, 208

Ogum, 25, 27, 29–32, 37, 59, 64, 74, 91–92, 94, 113, 120, 122, 129–130, 132, 145, 150, 154, 156, 160, 181, 185, 191, 193, 200–201, 204, 208

  Ogum Beira-Mar (Seaside Ogum), 92, 94, 113, 129

Olorún, 21, 34, 44, 127, 131, 152

omolucum, 104

Omulu, 19, 32–35, 59, 120, 129–130, 132, 150, 161, 181, 187, 191, 208, 212–213

Opelé de Ifá, 134

Orientals, 9, 13, 67–68, 120, 128, 130, 156

Orixás, 0, 9–10, 12–14, 16, 18, 21–41, 43–48, 53, 55, 58–59, 64, 68, 71, 73–74, 77–86, 91–97, 101–103, 106, 108–109, 115, 117, 120–128, 132–137, 142, 146–150, 154–156, 159–161, 163–164, 172, 176–177, 179–180, 182, 184, 190–191, 194–195, 200, 203, 209

Os Eguns do Candomble, 76

Ossãe, 17, 36–40, 66, 120, 132, 147, 149–150, 161, 191, 199, 205–206, 212

ossé, 86

otás, 77, 92, 95, 97, 192, 196, 204, 207, 209

oti, 83

Oxaguiã, 25, 35, 182

Oxala, 23, 34–36, 41–44, 76, 91, 116–118, 121–122, 125, 128, 130, 137, 144–146, 150, 152, 156–157, 182, 188, 190, 196, 198, 200, 202, 204, 206–207, 209

Oxóssi, 25, 27, 32, 36–38, 41, 47, 64, 67, 75–76, 91, 102, 120, 122, 128, 150, 156, 176, 183–184, 186, 188, 190, 192, 197–199, 207, 211–212

Oxumarê, 34–35, 38, 41, 43–44, 46, 132, 184, 211

Oyó, 12, 79

padê, 82, 107
pai pequeno, 95
pai-de-santo, 48, 95, 151
pajé, 16, 20
Pajelança, 20, 76
Palmares (*see also* quilombo), 57, 63, 74
passes, 7, 84-85, 128, 142, 163–165, 202
patuá, 137
peji, 73, 85, 92–94, 97, 125
Peji-Gã, 86, 93
pembas, 3, 19, 50, 72, 82, 84, 90, 112, 117–120, 136–137
Pentacostalism, 18
Pernambuco, 17, 185, 202
persona, 24–25, 177–185
phalanxes, 9, 127
po pupa (*see also* dendê oil), 83
Pombas-Giras, 3, 16, 41, 57, 59, 74, 102, 127, 137, 150, 157
    Maria Padilha, 111, 114, 123, 132
    Sete Encruzilhadas, 57
pontos riscados, 84, 135, 137
Portugal, Fernandes, 13–14, 130
Positivism, xii
Pretos Velhos, 3, 13, 60–63, 67, 75, 82, 123–124, 127–129, 140–142, 157, 163, 165
Protestantism, 2, 18

Qabalistic, 13, 129
quilombo (*see also* Palmares), 57, 74
quitutes, 103–104
Quimbanda, xii, 2, 5, 8, 14–15, 19, 50, 91, 96, 125, 128–130
quitutes, 103–104

Ramos, Artur, 19
Ribeiro, José, 110, 125

Rio de Janeiro, 1, 3–4, 9, 14, 18–20, 26, 30, 74–76, 91–92, 94, 96–97, 129, 136–138, 165, 168, 171–172, 202
Rio Grande do Sul, 76
Rivail, Hippolite-León (*see also* Denizard *and* Kardec, Allan), 5
roça, 91
Rodrígues, Raimundo Nina, 19
Roman Catholicism, xii, 2–3, 9, 14, 18, 22, 26, 43, 88, 115, 162, 177, 184
roncó, 94, 97
ronda, 137
Ruta graveolens, 116, 194

Salvador, 12, 26, 91
Salve, xi, xiii, 169
Sanscrit, 8
Sansieveria ceylanica, 115, 200
Santeria, xii
São Paulo, 129
Saravá, xiii, 146
Semitic, 121
Senegal, 74, 186
Sergipe, 17, 185
seu, 131, 137, 151–152, 154, 163, 165
Sidagã, 83
shamanism, 17, 155
souls, 5, 33, 35, 51, 68, 70–74, 86, 90, 92, 112, 129–130, 133, 143, 151, 157, 179
spirit guide, 10–11, 18, 23, 68, 91, 159, 161
Spiritualism, xii, 6, 19
Spiritism, xii, 4–9, 14, 17, 19, 87–88, 92, 125, 129, 156
    Table Spiritism, 7
Spiritist Federation of Umbanda, 9
Spiritist Tent of Our Lady of Piety, 9
Spiritist Union of Umbanda, 9
Sudanese, 22
Supreme Law of Umbanda, 28

syncretism, 22, 26, 35, 39, 44, 46–48, 130, 134

Table Spiritism, *see* Spiritiam
tenda, 91
terreiro, 4, 12, 14, 22–24, 39, 52, 60, 64, 68–74, 78–80, 82–83, 85–86, 88–89, 91–94, 96–97, 102–103, 105–106, 110, 119, 125–126, 128, 134, 137, 142, 151, 154, 156, 163, 165, 177–178, 185, 192, 208, 211–212
Theosophy, 68, 76
  Theosophical Society, 76
tombo, 11
Tupi, 20, 67, 76

Umbanda, xii, 2, 4–5, 7–15, 17–19, 23, 28, 64–65, 67–68, 73–76, 78, 83–84, 87, 91, 96, 110, 119, 125–127, 129–130, 137–139, 145–146, 156–157, 163, 189, 202, 210, 222
  Carioca Umbanda, 129
  Esoteric Umbanda, 74, 129
  popular Umbanda, 129
  Umbanda Congress, 9
Undines, 76, 128, 156

Varanda, Jorge Alberto, 76
Velloso, Caetano, 5
Verger, Pierre, 19, 69, 76
Vodunsi, 83, 96
Vodunsi-hunja, 83
Voodoo, xii, 43, 191

Western Magickal Mystery Tradition, 13, 107, 126, 129, 137, 142, 144–145, 168
  Western Magick, 22, 126
Western Occultism, 84, 192, 204, 206
Wicca (*see also* Witchcraft), xii, 107–108
Willis, Courtney, 136
Witchcraft (*see also* Wicca), 9, 17, 88, 130, 187, 189–192, 195, 203

Xampanã, 33, 181
Xangô, 12, 20, 25, 33, 40–41, 43–47, 64, 78–79, 96, 122, 128, 132, 150, 157, 160, 185, 190, 198, 201, 208–209
Xavier, Chico, 2

Yoruba, 12, 21–22, 39–40, 73, 95–97, 105, 158, 165–166, 178–182, 184

Zambi (*see also* Olórun), 9, 34, 60, 90–91, 110, 144–146
Zanzibar, 119

STAY IN TOUCH. . .

Llewellyn publishes hundreds of products on your favorite subjects.

On the following page you will find listed some products now available on related subjects. Your local bookstore stocks most of these and will stock new Llewellyn titles as they become available. We urge your patronage.

Order by Phone

Call toll-free within the U.S. and Canada, 1–800–THE MOON.
In Minnesota call (612) 291–1970.
We accept Visa, MasterCard, and American Express.

Order by Mail

Send the full price of your order (MN residents add 7% sales tax) in U.S. funds to:

> Llewellyn Worldwide
> P.O. Box 64383, Dept. K235-6
> St. Paul, MN 55164–0383, U.S.A.

Postage and Handling

- $4.00 for orders $15.00 and under
- $5.00 for orders over $15.00
- No charge for orders over $100.00

We ship UPS in the continental United States. We cannot ship to P.O. boxes. Orders shipped to Alaska, Hawaii, Canada, Mexico, and Puerto Rico will be sent first-class mail.

International orders: Airmail—add freight equal to price of each book to the total price of order, plus $5.00 for each non-book item (audiotapes, etc.). Surface mail—Add $1.00 per item.

Allow 4–6 weeks delivery on all orders. Postage and handling rates subject to change.

Group Discounts

We offer a 20% quantity discount to group leaders or agents. You must order a minimum of 5 copies of the same book or product to get our special quantity price.

FREE CATALOG

Get a free copy of our color catalog, *New Worlds of Mind and Spirit*. Subscribe for just $10.00 in the United States and Canada ($20.00 overseas, first class mail). Many bookstores carry *New Worlds*—ask for it!

THE TAROT OF THE ORISHAS

Created by Zolrak
Illustrated by Durkon

This remarkable system employs, for the first time ever, the powerful energies of Brazilian Candomble—the spiritist religion that originated with the Yoruba people of west-central Africa. Considered by many to be far more powerful for magic and divination than the traditional tarot, The Tarot of the Orishas taps into the pure, sacred, potent energy of the supernatural beings called the Orishas.

Book: A bilingual (English and Spanish), in-depth guide to the meanings of The Tarot of the Orishas cards. Describes how to use the cards for divination, magic or meditation, including four unique layouts especially designed for use with this deck.

1-56718-844-3, 360 pp., 6 x 9, illus., softcover $14.95

Deck: Breathtaking, full-color cards which depict the Orishas, the four elements, and symbols such as Karma and the Custodian Angel. Cards incorporate numerology, astrology and other branches of metaphysics. Cards in English, Spanish and Portuguese; instruction booklet in English and Spanish.

1-56718-843-5
77 full-color cards, 64 pp. instruction booklet $19.95

Ritual Layout Sheet: Full-color ritual sheet illustrating the cosmic energies of the universe. Use for the card layouts described in The Tarot of the Orishas book or for traditional layouts.

1-56718-845-1
Ritual layout sheet , 8 pp. instruction booklet $7.89

Kit: A boxed set that includes the book, the deck, the instruction booklet, and as a bonus, the full-color ritual layout sheet.

1-56718-842-7
• 77 full-color cards in English, Spanish and Portuguese
• 64 pp. instruction booklet in English and Spanish
• 6 x 9, 360 pp. illus. softcover book in English and Spanish
• Ritual layout sheet with 8 pp. instruction booklet $32.95

To order, call 1–800–THE MOON
Prices subject to change without notice.